the ST. LAWRENCE

the
ST. LAWRENCE

Henry Beston

Illustrated by **A.Y. JACKSON**

With a New Introduction by **Daniel G. Payne**

OXFORD
UNIVERSITY PRESS

OXFORD
UNIVERSITY PRESS

Oxford University Press is a department of the University of Oxford.
It furthers the University's objective of excellence in research, scholarship,
and education by publishing worldwide. Oxford is a registered trade mark of
Oxford University Press in the UK and in certain other countries.

Published in Canada by
Oxford University Press
8 Sampson Mews, Suite 204,
Don Mills, Ontario M3C 0H5

www.oupcanada.com

Library and Archives Canada Cataloguing in Publication

Beston, Henry, 1888–1968
The St. Lawrence / Henry Beston.

(Wynford project)
Includes index.
ISBN 978-0-19-544955-6

1. Beston, Henry, 1888–1968—Travel—Saint Lawrence River.
2. Saint Lawrence River—Description and travel. I. Title. II. Series:
Wynford Project

FC2754.3.B48 2012   917.1404'3   C2011-907207-6

Cover image: ©Ian Coristine / 1000IslandsPhotoArt.com

Interior illustrations by A.Y. Jackson: Courtesy of the Estate of the late Dr. Naomi Jackson Groves

Printed and bound in the United States of America.

1 2 3 4 — 15 14 13 12

Introduction to the Wynford Edition

Daniel G. Payne

In 1937 the publishing house of Farrar & Rinehart released *Kennebec: Cradle of Americans* by the Maine poet Robert P. Tristram Coffin as the inaugural volume in the Rivers of America series, conceived by Canadian novelist and historian Constance Lindsay Skinner. Skinner's plan for the Rivers of America was an ambitious one: a sequence of twenty-four books on the great rivers of North America each written and illustrated by prominent writers and artists who had a vital connection to the region. Skinner was determined that the series would not simply be a collection of travelogues but enduring works of literature that portrayed the rivers as living entities shaping the land and cultures they touched. Although Skinner died in 1939 while editing the sixth book in the series, Carl Carmer's *The Hudson*, her visionary project exceeded even her aspirations: it eventually grew to sixty-five titles published over a period of thirty-seven years.

Through works such as *The Outermost House* (1928) and *Herbs and the Earth* (1935), Henry Beston had already established a reputation as one of America's pre-eminent nature writers when he agreed to write a volume for the Rivers of America series. Beston chose to write about the St. Lawrence, the great river dividing Canada from the United States, situated approximately 322 kilometres north of his farm in Nobleboro, Maine. The resulting work, *The St. Lawrence* (1942), was one of Beston's most multi-facted literary projects; as the distinguished literary critic Sherman Paul notes, "it is at once a guide book, a children's book (when historical events, Indian captivities, and legends are recounted), and a nature book."[1] The artist chosen to illustrate *The St. Lawrence* was the renowned Canadian painter A.Y. Jackson, a founding member of the Group of Seven, whose paintings inspired by the Canadian landscape are generally considered to be part of Canada's first major national art movement.

There was relatively little in Henry Beston's early life that foreshadowed a strong interest in natural history or the outdoors. Born Henry Edouard Sheahan (he began using the name Henry Beston in his early thirties) in 1888 to a French mother and Irish-American father, he grew up in Quincy, Massachusetts, where his father practised as a physician. His mother died when Beston was still a boy, and his father died a few years later, shortly after he had begun his first year of study at Harvard University. Following his graduation from Harvard with a master's degree in literature in 1909, he spent a year teaching at the Université de Lyons in France. This period was important, Beston later wrote, because rural France was "the first place in which I encountered and knew and loved the earth."[2] This may not have been quite true in a literal sense—as a boy he spent summers in the country with his mother as well as a great deal of time on the water at the Quincy seashore—but it was in pre-war France where he had his first revelatory experience with the "peasant's earth," the rural, working life tied closely to the cyclical rhythms of nature.

When the First World War began, Beston's sympathies were entirely with the Entente, so he eagerly volunteered to serve as an ambulance driver in France.

Beston's time on the Western Front, which included service at the horrific battle of Verdun, dispelled whatever romantic notions about war that he may have once held. Although he greatly admired the soldiers and sailors with whom he served, Beston came to believe that modern industrial civilization was detrimental to the human spirit, creating a faithless, more violent, "artificial" man.[3] His first book, A Volunteer Poilu (1916), described his service as an ambulance driver, an experience that was shared by a number of men who went on to distinguished literary careers (the most famous of whom is Ernest Hemingway). Although Beston spent more time at the front than most of these literary volunteers of the American Field Service, he is rarely mentioned in the context of A Volunteer Poilu. Indeed, few critics recognize that the book's author, Henry Sheahan, is the same writer who would later gain literary fame under the name Henry Beston. Later, when the United States entered the war in 1917, he took a position as a war correspondent serving with the US Navy.

After the war, Beston took to writing fairy tales as an attempt to counter the effect of the war. Writing to his friend the Reverend J. Luther Neff, Beston explained his new interest in this way: "Weary of Armageddon, I fled as far away from it as I could."[4] Although these stories were immensely popular with young readers (including the children of his close friend Theodore Roosevelt Jr.), Beston felt that he had more to offer as a writer than journalism and children's stories: "If you can write and don't," he said, "something within you withers & dies, and with its death envenoms the soul."[5] During the early 1920s Beston also served as editor of The Living Age and wrote a number of magazine articles and an engaging collection of biographical sketches entitled The Book of Gallant Vagabonds (1925). Still, he was plagued with the unsettling sense that he was approaching mid-life and had yet to truly find his voice as a writer.

In September 1926, the thirty-eight-year-old Beston left Quincy to spend a two-week vacation in Cape Cod, where he had built a shack he named the Fo'castle on an isolated stretch of dunes overlooking the Atlantic Ocean near Eastham. As he later wrote in The Outermost House:

> I went there to spend a fortnight in September. The fortnight ending, I lingered on, and as the year lengthened into autumn, the beauty and mystery of this earth and outer sea so possessed me that I could not go. The world to-day is sick to its thin blood for lack of elemental things, for fire before the hands, for water welling from the earth, for air, for the dear earth itself underfoot. In my world of beach and dune these elemental presences lived and had their being, and under their arch there moved an incomparable pageant of nature and the year. . . . The longer I stayed, the more eager was I to know this coast and to share the mysterious and elemental life.[6]

On the great beach, Beston refined his ideas regarding the harmful effect that rampant industrialism and its by-products had on humankind: dulling our senses, increasing our proclivity toward violence, and distancing us from the rhythms of the earth in both a physical and spiritual way. Perhaps his boldest assertion was a challenge to the anthropocentric belief that humans were of a different order than the rest of creation: "We need another and a wiser and perhaps a more mystical concept of animals.... They are not brethren, they are not underlings; they are other nations, caught with ourselves in the net of life and time, fellow prisoners of the splendour and travail of the earth."[7] Both contemporary reviewers and modern critics have praised *The Outermost House*, which is universally considered to be one of the great classics of American nature writing. Thomas Lyon, the editor of *This Incomperable Lande: A Book of American Nature Writing*, compares *The Outermost House* to Thoreau's *Walden* and Edward Abbey's *Desert Solitaire*, aptly calling it a "talismanic book of solitude."[8]

In 1929 Beston married Elizabeth Coatsworth, a poet and writer whose *The Cat Who Went to Heaven* won the 1931 Newbery Medal for excellence in children's literature. Beston moved to Hingham, Massachusetts, a south shore village some 32 kilometres south of Boston, where Coatsworth and her mother lived in a lovely old sea captain's house; there they soon had two daughters, Margaret and Catherine. To follow up on the success of *The Outermost House*, Beston signed a contract with Doubleday to write a second book about Cape Cod, one examining life on the inner shore. He soon found, however, that Hingham was not nearly so conducive to writing about nature as his dune shack on the beach had been, complaining that "there is no nature here to see, there are no birds save the spotted Chevrolet and the Greater and Lesser Buick."[9] He eventually abandoned the book about the inner cape, reluctantly concluding that it would not measure up to the standard he had set with *The Outermost House*.

Beston was not a prolific writer; he wrote slowly, eschewing the clattering of the typewriter, preferring instead to use pencil and paper so the noise of the machine would not interfere with the sound of his sentences. What Beston may have sacrificed in quantity, however, he made up with quality—as a prose stylist, his work is exemplary; his books and essays are models of clear, concise writing. Few writers have managed to capture the rhythms of the English language as lyrically as did Beston, whose work can be seen as a prose corollary to William Carlos Williams's celebration of the American idiom in his poetry. Indeed, many of the writers who most appreciated the lyrical beauty of Beston's work were poets, one of whom was Sylvia Plath, who stayed at the Fo'castle with her husband Ted Hughes in 1957 and paid tribute to Beston in her poem "The Hermit at Outermost House."

While visiting friends in Maine in 1931, Beston learned that an old farm on Damariscotta Lake in Nobleboro was for sale. As his wife later recalled, "He who might hesitate for hours on the choice of a few words, could make up his mind on the future course of his life in an instant."[10] At the place he and his family called Chimney Farm, Beston once again found the literary inspiration from nature that produced his best work. He now demonstrated a growing belief that farm life was a possible counterweight to the toxic effects of a modern world that was "without a truly human past and may be without a human future."[11] In his later works, most notably *Herbs and the Earth* (1935), *The St. Lawrence* (1942), and *Northern Farm* (1948), Beston continued to call for a revitalized link between nature and humankind. At times Beston's work sounds like a nostalgic brand of neo-agrarianism in its romantic appreciation of rural life, but at other times his critique of modern civilization still seems remarkably current in a world where the inculcation of consumerist culture on a global scale has seemingly done little but create a more violent, materialistic, and pessimistic humankind yearning for hope and spiritual solace.

The outbreak of the Second World War reinforced Beston's bleakest predictions about the trajectory of humankind in the twentieth century. The keystone to our well-being as individuals and as a species, he believed, was in reclaiming our humanity by reconnecting with the cycle of the seasons, the sky above us, the waters around us, and the earth beneath our feet. In the foreword to the 1949 edition of *The Outermost House*, he wrote:

> Once again, I set down the core of what I continue to believe. Nature is a part of our humanity, and without some awareness and experience of that divine mystery man ceases to be man. When the Pleiades and the wind in the grass are no longer a part of the human spirit, a part of very flesh and bone, man becomes, as it were, a kind of cosmic outlaw, having neither the completeness and integrity of the animal nor the birthright of a true humanity. As I once said elsewhere, "Man can either be less than man or more than man, and both are monsters, the last more dread."[12]

Throughout Beston's books and articles he continually seeks to share his sense of the splendor, mystery, and poetry of the earth; the role of nature as an integral part of the human spirit; and the healing power of nature. He pointedly contrasts the natural, regenerative rhythms of the earth to the wanton destruction he attributed to industrial society—as he would state many times in his acerbic commentaries on the modern world, he took *his* stand "on the side of life."

In writing *The St. Lawrence* Beston was entirely in accord with Constance Lindsay Skinner's original vision for the series (although since her untimely death in 1939 the Rivers of America was now edited by her successors, Stephen Vincent Benét and Carl Carmer), while building upon his recurring themes about man's disconnect from nature, which created a more violent, self-destructive world. In *The St. Lawrence*, therefore, Beston sought to draw a distinction between industrial society and its effects upon the land, the human spirit, and those cultures throughout the river's history that had a more vital, sustainable connection to the natural world. Beston succinctly contrasts these differing approaches early in *The St. Lawrence*: "The industrial age has so covered the face of the earth with negative dirt, with wreckage, pollution, and yahoo squalor, that I find it a relief now and then to discover myself in dirt of a positive kind. By positive dirt, I mean such dirt as one may find about an open market place, even such dirt as has something to do with living."[13]

In his research for the book, Beston travelled extensively throughout Quebec and the Canadian Maritimes to get a feel for the people and history of the region and "the almost timeless forces of nature neighboring the river and its coasts."[14] His original intent was not to write a social history of the Laurentian region, but rather to write an ecological history, stating in the book's preface: "I have tried first and foremost to keep my eyes on the river itself. It is not a chronological or anecdotal history of Laurentian Canada; where men and events appear in these pages they have seemed to me to have a living relation to the river."[15] As Beston knew, however, the ecological history of the St. Lawrence was closely tied to the human settlements along the river, and the ways in which those communities treated the river and the land of the region varied widely.

The earliest inhabitants of the Laurentian region were Aboriginal people, and Beston's deeply held beliefs in the value of a spiritual life tied to the earth's rhythms were reflected in his long-standing interest in the Aboriginal peoples of the Americas.[16] In *The St. Lawrence* Beston drew a vivid contrast between the Aboriginal people's perception of nature and that of the European settlers who supplanted them in the region. Despite these differences, he asserts that at least in French Canada Aboriginal people had left a significant cultural legacy, stating, "The Algonquin has influenced the habitant farmers far more than he has the Yankee yeoman across the great frontier."[17] In a fascinating chapter on captivity narratives, Beston draws attention to the large number of white captives who made a conscious decision not to return to their colonial settlements when the opportunity arose, asserting that

> whether they knew it or not, they were at peace with the tense American earth. The white civilization of their inheritance was at war with the earth. . . . The Indians made no such war. They made room for themselves in nature, but it was to their interest to let nature remain what it was. The earth was an ancestral mystery. Across it like the fugitive wind moved the direct and vivid pattern of their lives.[18]

Beston devotes many pages in *The St. Lawrence* to the Aboriginal way of life and points out that there is still a vast northern wilderness in Canada "that has as little to do with law and the white spirit as a billow of sleet in a gale. It is the Indian's America."[19] It was a vision of North America that held sway in only a relatively few and remote places and was steadily losing ground, however grudgingly, to the modern world.

As Beston saw it, there was one era in the history of the St. Lawrence—"le vieux Canada," French Canada's "golden age" of the nineteenth century—that seemed to offer a sustainable alternative to the modern era. There is, therefore, a deeply melancholic aspect to Beston's thrilling chapter on the siege of Quebec and the fall of French Canada. Scattered throughout the old quarters of Quebec City, he writes, "One wanders by Norman roofs, with Norman gables and Norman chimneys, relics of a past when human beings would seem to have come into the world with a sense of beauty as naturally as they arrived with a right hand."[20] Much of contemporary Quebec City, he observes, is "a place of business now, carried on in rather grim buildings of the gaslit age, a town of wharves, narrow streets, small factories, filling stations, and stores with bright paint and dirty windows," with a "commercialism . . . more British in core than French."[21] In antiquated parts of the city, however, one was still able to catch glimpses of what Beston believed was "the genuine and little appreciated key to the spirit of the place. In a way, it is key to much one encounters in French

Canada. Passing these old houses, these windows filled with books, religious manuals, and objects of Catholic devotion, it comes upon me again that this city has little to do with either the seventeenth or the eighteenth century, but everything to do with a particularly characteristic and romantically complete period of the nineteenth."[22] Beston often returns to this idea as the linchpin to understanding the relationship between the people and the land of the St. Lawrence region. The isolation of the St. Lawrence valley had created a people who loved and honoured the land, and their efforts to earn a living from nature

> had created something unique. On its green and northern banks it pre-
> sented to history a long mid-nineteenth century idyll of earth and man.
> In all North American history there has been only one such unified, com-
> plete and picturesque adventure in living. Between the eighteenth century
> and the hideous industrial perversion "le vieux Canada" stands as a kind
> of triumph, unpretending and patient, of the mystery and spirit of man.[23]

While Beston pointedly contrasts the French-Canadians' relationship to the land with what he saw as the Anglo-American drive to subjugate and control nature, he was forced to concede that there were some regrettable similarities, citing "the savage business" of pulpwood logging as one example. Beston excoriates *le pulp* as "a commerce of pure destruction thoroughly bad in the long run for the psyche of any people. So far there seems little relation between the cutting and any rhythm of forest growth. Nature is there to be sacked and the fierce attack goes on." He goes on to say in a tone that seems inspired more by desperate hope than of conviction,

> Time and the spirit of man, I think, have turned against this pattern of the
> world. Sooner or later, guided by its own intelligence or by bitter necessity,
> a civilization will again remember that visible nature is not the immediate
> spoil of an age or its generations, but the timeless inheritance of man, the
> ancient mystery to be forever shared with those who forever are to come.[24]

Earlier in the book, Beston stated that "for all his redoubtable prowess with the ax [the French-Canadian] was at peace with his earth and his fields" in a way that Americans were not.[25] As he travelled downriver, however, Beston was forced to concede that modern industrialism had left its mark in the St. Lawrence region as it had everywhere else:

> Of the industrialism—largely absentee in ownership—which has become
> a part of the river I had best again hold my peace. It is industrialism as
> it is everywhere, a belittler of man and a destroyer of his living relation
> to the earth. . . . There is one destruction which is of God, and that is the
> destruction inherent in the renewal of life; the dead leaf must wither and
> crumble in the cold, the flower give way to the relentless pressure of the
> seed below. Opposed to this is another destruction which is of the Devil,
> a destruction without necessity and without creative future, a destruction

only conceivable in age of the emptiness of the human spirit, and working itself out in brutality and the ruin of the heritage of men. Of this the earth is full, the smoke of the torment ascending, and it will need all the trumpets of Revelation to restore to us the earth which men have loved.[26]

Despite the end of "the golden age of *les anciens*" and the encroachment of industrialism on the St. Lawrence, Beston was still able to find a hopeful sign in the surviving remnants of Old Canada scattered throughout the region. There were places still where the manners and customs of the region were maintained: "Encountering the enchantments of progress, it has modified itself, adjusting itself to the chaos as best it can. Here it has succumbed or retreated, here it has made its compromise, here it has accepted the change as one might take a recommended but unpalatable dose."[27]

On November 12, 1942, Farrar released *The St. Lawrence* to excellent reviews, and within just a few months the first printing had been completely sold out. Farrar had to hurry through a second printing. A pocket-sized edition for the Armed Service was also published, making the book available to thousands of service men and women overseas. As one reviewer noted, "The Canada of *The St. Lawrence* is a welcome and appropriate contribution of North America which the series is building," going on to praise Beston's "lyric treatment of Canadian nature."[28] In Marine Leland's "French Canada: An Example of What America is Learning," an article that appeared in the May 1945 issue of *The Modern Language Journal*, Leland also praised the book, writing: "Culturally speaking, French Canada is as individualized and independent as any other American country. Henry Beston, in . . . *The St. Lawrence*, describes French Canada with succinct accuracy."[29]

In Beston's later years his work consistently found an appreciative critical and popular audience. Although he wrote just one more major work after *The St. Lawrence*—*Northern Farm*, published in 1948—he published a popular anthology of Maine writing, *White Pine and Blue Water: A State of Maine Reader* in 1950. His earlier children's stories also enjoyed a renaissance when they were collected and republished as *Henry Beston's Fairy Tales* in 1952. As Beston's health declined over the last ten years of his life, he was cheered by numerous literary accolades, including several honorary degrees, and in 1960 he became the third recipient (the first two were T.S. Eliot and Robert Frost) of the American Academy of Arts and Sciences' Emerson-Thoreau Award. Perhaps the most gratifying honour came in 1964, three years after the creation of the Cape Cod National Seashore (CCNS). At a well-attended ceremony held at the park's new visitor centre (located just a few kilometres from Beston's old dune shack), *The Outermost House* was designated a National Literary Landmark and cited as one of the inspirations leading to the creation of the CCNS. After a series of debilitating strokes, Henry Beston died at his beloved Chimney Farm in 1968. Ten years later—fifty years after the publication of *The Outermost House*—the Fo'castle was washed out to sea during an immense winter storm, a fate that would undoubtedly been seen as fitting by the man who had written, "To understand this great outer beach . . . one must have a sense of it as the scene of wreck and elemental disaster."

As his writing career wound down, Beston sometimes expressed concern that he would be remembered for just one book, *The Outermost House*. While this work certainly stands out as a truly remarkable literary achievement, most literary critics (and readers) would probably agree with Sherman Paul, who writes in *For Love of the World: Essays on Nature Writers*, "Beston should figure for us as a writer of several works, not just *The Outermost House*." In recent years several of these books, including *Herbs and the Earth, Northern Farm, Especially Maine: The Natural World of Henry Beston from Cape Cod to the St. Lawrence, Henry Beston's Fairy Tales*—and now *The St. Lawrence*—have been published in new editions. Many of the primary themes in Beston's work—such as challenging anthropocentric perspectives concerning nature; the importance of establishing a connection with place; the link between the cycles of nature and humankind's yearning for a spiritual connection with the world; and the dangers presented by our industrial, consumerist culture—all maintain their relevance today and are evident in the work of outstanding modern writers such as Rachel Carson, Edward Abbey, Wendell Berry, Terry Tempest Williams, and Barry Lopez.

Despite his recurring pessimism about the effect of industrialized society on the human spirit—and he probably would not have been particularly impressed with our post-industrial consumerist society, either—were Beston to return to the St. Lawrence region today he might well find some cause for optimism. In retracing his travels along the northern shore of the river, he would see that while many of the farms along the St. Lawrence have given way to communities no longer tied so closely to agriculture, a remarkable number of the residents maintain small vegetable gardens in their backyards. He would note with approval the pride taken in regional cuisine using locally grown foods. Perhaps most of all, he would have rejoiced that the spectacular annual migration of water fowl that he describes so beautifully in *The St. Lawrence* still continues, with the birds now afforded some protection in sanctuaries along the river such as Cap Tourmente National Wildlife Refuge in the Charlevoix region of Quebec. In these things Beston would find hope for the future of the land still maintained by people along the river: "It lives on, no ghost, because its values live, and these, I think, will not die until a last Ave is said at the ploughing, and the last of the great mill wheels, ceasing its noble thundering and plashing, stops forever on its Laurentian hill."[30]

Notes

1. Paul, *For Love of the World*, 116.
2. Beston, *Especially Maine*, 48.
3. Beston, *The Outermost House*, 165–66.
4. Beston to Reverend J. Luther Neff, 12 August 1919.
5. Beston to unidentified correspondent (probably Jake Day), 1 February 1921.
6. Beston, *The Outermost House*, 10–11.
7. Ibid., 19–20.
8. Lyon, *This Incomperable Lande*, 83.

9. Beston, *Especially Maine*, 72.
10. Ibid., 6.
11. Beston, *Herbs and the Earth*, 5.
12. Beston, *The Outermost House*, xxxv.
13. Beston, *The St. Lawrence*, 25.
14. Ibid., ix.
15. Ibid.
16. Beston wrote two short books on the American Indians, *The Sons of Kai* (1926) based on a Navaho legend and *A Glimpse of the Indian Past* (1946) about the Indians native to Cape Cod.
17. Beston, *The St. Lawrence*, 159.
18. Ibid., 43–44.
19. Ibid., 247.
20. Ibid., 18.
21. Ibid., 19.
22. Ibid.
23. Ibid., 94.
24. Ibid., 155.
25. Ibid., 107.
26. Ibid., 169, 172.
27. Ibid., 108.
28. Naeseth, review of *Chicago* and *The St. Lawrence*, 106.
29. Leland, "French Canada," 393.
30. Beston, *The St. Lawrence*, 109.

References

Beston, Henry. *Especially Maine: The Natural World of Henry Beston from Cape Cod to the St. Lawrence*. 1970. Reprint Brattleboro, Vermont: The Stephen Greene Press, 1976.

Beston, Henry. *Herbs and the Earth*. Boston: David R. Godine, Publisher, 1990. First published 1935 by Doubleday, Doran, and Company.

Beston, Henry. Letter to Morton Smith, 22 June 1938. Beston Family Archives. Bowdoin College, Brunswick, Maine.

Beston, Henry. Letter to Reverend J. Luther Neff, 12 August 1919. Beston Family Archives, Bowdoin College, Brunswick, Maine.

Beston, Henry. Letter to unidentified correspondent (probably Jake Day), 1 February 1921. Beston Family Archives. Bowdoin College, Brunswick, Maine.

Beston, Henry. *The Outermost House: A Year of Life on the Great Beach of Cape Cod*. New York: Henry Holt, 1988. First published 1928 by Doubleday.

Beston, Henry. *The St. Lawrence*. New York: Farrar and Rinehart, 1942.

Leland, Marine. "French Canada: An Example of What America Is Learning." *The Modern Language Journal* 29, no. 5 (May 1945): 389–402.

Lyon, Thomas. *This Incomperable Lande: A Book of American Nature Writing*. New York: Penguin, 1991.

Naeseth, Henriette C.K. Review of *The Chicago* by Harry Hansen and *The St. Lawrence* by Henry Beston. *The Mississippi Valley Historical Review* 30, no. 1 (June 1943): 105–6.

Paul, Sherman. *For Love of the World: Essays on Nature Writers*. Iowa City: University of Iowa Press, 1992.

Publisher's Note

The St. Lawrence was first published in 1942. This facsimile edition faithfully reproduces the original text of the first edition. In the seven decades since, society's attitudes toward Canada's First Nations peoples and indeed the very terms used to denote those societies have changed greatly. So have historical views of first contact between Europeans and the First Nations. *The St. Lawrence* is, like any creative work, an artifact of its time, and it is only fair to say that the twenty-first century reader may stumble across the occasional expression no longer in common use.

To the Abbé Albert Tessier

WHO GUARDS AND CHERISHES
THE INHERITANCE OF HIS PEOPLE

Preface

In writing this book I have tried first and foremost to keep my eyes on the river itself. It is not a chronological or anecdotal history of Laurentian Canada; where men and events appear in these pages they have seemed to me to have a living relation to the river. I have divided the book in the following manner: the first third is concerned with the past, the second with the present, and the last third with the almost timeless forces of nature neighboring the river and its coasts. The reader will find that the book largely concerns itself with the French regions of the St. Lawrence, for there is the river at its greatest and there is human life most shaped by its presence and influences. Perhaps above all what I have tried to give is a sense of the St. Lawrence as a part of the scale and vastness of our North America.

Living in eastern Maine and scarce two hundred miles from what we all call "the line", I have long been familiar with the river and its people. The uninhabited range of the frontier separates our completely different worlds but the north which is our common inheritance makes us neighbors. The world of Katahdin and the white pine and the world of the Mont Ste. Anne and the dense spruce both know what it is like when the northeaster darkens the already darkened twilight with the thickening onrush of the snow.

During the course of these last few years, I have

sought out many to each side of the line and wish to thank them here for the courtesy and particular good will with which they gave me every help and aid. Village curés of the river parishes, university scholars, busy librarians, officials at Ottawa and Quebec, boatmen, eel-catchers, farmers, and woodcutters—how friendly they all were. Beginning at home, I wish to thank my wife, Elizabeth Coatsworth Beston, my companion in so many of these adventures, for her unfailing help and wisest counsel, for her encouragement and her adventurous willingness to try the road ahead. I wish to thank my friend the Abbé Albert Tessier who welcomed me to the river and gave me the letters and good counsel which opened so many a door. I would thank my friend Dr. D. A. Déry of Quebec, founder of the Société Provancher—the society which preserves and studies the great world of nature on the river; to him and to his scientific knowledge so genially and freely given I confess a very great obligation. I would thank my friend Miss Hazel Boswell of Quebec for sharing with me her profound and sympathetic insight into the spirit of the habitant world and its legends; I would thank my friend Mrs. Carroll White (born Mlle. Le Moyne and now seigneuresse of her hereditary island) for a world of most interesting details concerning the epic of the wheat and the traditional pattern of life on the river, and without the kindness of my old friend Philip Robb Esqre. I should never have got certain material which I required to complete the story of eeling on the coast.

I owe, as so many do who study the popular arts of Canada, a debt to the scholarship and kindness of

PREFACE

M. Marius Barbeau of the National Museum at Ottawa. I would thank again Father Doucet of Bersimis for his most generous hospitality. And let me not forget the anonymous young deck hand who told me the poignant fable of the legend of the Northern Lights.

The chapter on birds has been set down in a most informal manner and is meant to be read in the same mood. A formal study of the bird-life of the lower river would require the best of a lifetime and a dozen books. I wish to acknowledge here a particular debt to Mr. Harrison F. Lewis, Chief Federal Migratory Bird Officer of the Dominion of Canada, adviser and ally of every student of Canadian bird-life; it is to his kindness that I owe a first listing of the birds of the lower St. Lawrence.

One last small explanation. The "north shore" is approximately the country between the Cap Tourmente and the few parishes just to the east of the Saguenay; the "Côte Nord" is the wild country beginning more or less with the Portneuf River and extending eastward and northerly towards the great waters of the Gulf of St. Lawrence.

To Morton and Margaret Coatsworth Smith I owe my treasured opportunity to write a number of these chapters in the peace and quiet of a study put generously at my disposal. I would thank them with all my heart.

And now *en avant*, and to the River.

HENRY BESTON

Chimney Farm
Nobleboro, Maine

Contents

Contents

1
Ontario to Montreal

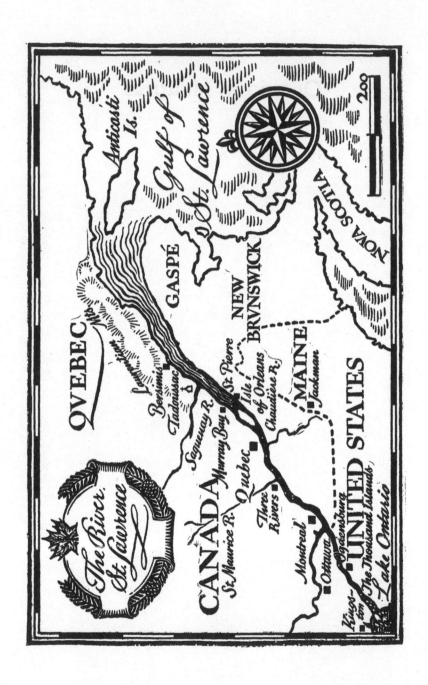

The River St. Lawrence

QUEBEC
CANADA
GASPÉ
Anticosti Is.
Gulf of St. Lawrence
NOVA SCOTIA
NEW BRUNSWICK
MAINE
UNITED STATES
Laurentian Mts.
Bersimis
Tadoussac
Saguenay R.
Murray Bay
Quebec
St. Maurice R.
Three Rivers
Montreal
Ottawa
Kingston
Ogdensburg
The Thousand Islands
Lake Ontario
St. Pierre
Isle of Orleans
Chaudiere R.
Jackman

200

UNDER a vast land sky, milky-pale with a universal tissue of cloud, the great fresh-water sea rolls before the west wind towards the narrowing and approaching shores which begin the river. The pale waves of Ontario diminish as the wind crowds them into the St. Lawrence, and a thunderstorm of early afternoon touches the dark American green of the nearer woods with silver and a veil of rain. Save for the gulls who follow beside the ship, there seem few birds.

In its great departure, the river is itself something of another lake, flowing in vague and enormous motion to the east. Indeed the whole rhythm of the landscape has an eastward resolution, with its tree shapes and its tree boughs streaming backward, and the river itself moving eastward below both current and wave. Shores of fields and hardwoods in their midsummer greenery presently gather a blacker and old-fashioned wildness, and the stream surprisingly becomes a whole inland sea of fanciful isles and archipelagoes. The Thousand Islands (the phrase has touched the American imagination) are here for the counting. Some are mere rocks emerging from the stream, poising one resolute small tree in a crevice of grey stone, some are rural felicities

3

of field and tree with the river as a moat, others are solitaries set apart, each like a lonely star. The houses which crown them are the comfortable houses of a comfortable past, but here and there one ventures into a realm of turreted and shingled castles which is fairy land as the American fancy of the seventies and eighties saw it with perhaps a little help from Tennyson. Currents stir in the seeming lake, flowing visibly between the isles: the river is gaining strength. At the water's edge, on polished shelves of stone, gatherings of the common tern stand massed in feathered whiteness, sheltering from the wind.

These waters might cover the entire earth so much do they seem without definition or bound. A narrow passage ultimately leads from them into the next great phase of the stream.

It is the York State St. Lawrence, the river with Ontario and Britain to one side, and the United States and Congress and the presidents to the other. To the Canadian north are old farms and fields with willows bordering their shores and silvering in the wind. Here and there, in crannies of the bank under a decorum of leaves, are old-fashioned cottages playful with architectural gingerbread, and from time to time appear small rustic towns whose houses and trees seem to have been planted together in some Canadian moment of the mid-Victorian mood. The landscape reflects a way of life less hurried than the American. Town halls have even something of a British propriety, and the bells in the

brick churches strike noon with a measured and English air.

Across the stream, under the same inland light, the
same level distances of grassland and trees fall back
from the yellow earth of the New York shore. The
farms seem more scattered and uneven and are farther
from the river, towns count for less, and there are more
groves of elms standing green beside the bank. It is not
the landscape of the shores, however, which now seizes
upon the imagination of the traveler. For thirty miles
he has been following a great and single channel direct
as some vast canal, a line of water drawn across a part
of North America as it might be across the face of
Mars. So evenly between its banks does it keep its aver-
age width of a fair two miles that the long, natural
perspective has even something of an artificial air; one
might be in the presence of some great work of the ancient and mysterious America of the Mound Builders.
Looking westward from Prescott in Ontario one sees a
surprising sight at the far end of the fairway. It is a
sealike horizon on a river, a level line of water and sky
suspended in space between the substantiality of parallel shores, themselves vanishing over the rounding
plunge of earth.

Flat wavelets speckle the channel, flicked from the
current by the inland breeze. Eastward and ahead, vast
steps in the rush of the river downhill from the lakes,
lie the great rapids, the roar of their narrow caldrons,
long slopes, and wider seas of fury soon to break upon
the listening ear.

Only the strong current, eddying in deep mid-channel and flowing like a long and hastening ripple past the banks, carries a hint of what is presently to come. The river has quickened pace into new country, an open tableland of grass and gravel down whose yellow banks glacial boulders have here and there rolled to the water's edge; the great main channel is over and done; ahead, level islands of the stream's own making bar and turn it in its gathering and meandering rush. It is farming land, and there are cattle on the islands, black-and-white Holsteins feeding under the willows and the grovelike beauty of the elms. A touch or two of industrialism on the Canadian side, and the beginning there of the canal world does not change the character of the landscape or the emphasis of its way of life. The river, which at Prescott and Ogdensburg was a pale and inland blue, has in this yellower earth gathered a tinge of green.

Lake freighters coming and going to Montreal have gone into the canals. Slow dignities of hulk and painted iron, they move along the separate water, their stacks visible in the distance above and through the trees.

The islands are now close at hand, lying in the stream like hindrances in a corridor, and confusing the descent with turns and passages about and between their steeper-growing banks. Alongside, the water is now plunging forward in a rush, boiling up from below in circles like huge lily pads expanding. Two rapids which are little more than a new and fiercer hurrying under the keel pass by without drama of sight or sound. More rapids follows and a long rush at whose far end a growing roar overflows into the blue and casual day.

A shudder, a strange motion downhill into a vast confusion and a vaster sound, and one is in the pool which is the climax of the rapids of the Long Sault. So steep is the winding rush downslope into the pool and out of it along a furious curve that the rims of water close along the banks stand higher than the tumult in the pit, and one passes, as it were, through banks of water as well as banks of land. Currents and agitations of wind, rapids of the invisible air, enclose the ship in a leap, scurrying the deck with their small and wild unrest. In the caldrons all is giant and eternal din, a confusion and war and leaping-up of white water in every figure and fury of its elemental being, the violence roaring in a ceaseless and universal hue and cry of water in all its sounds and tongues. The forms of water rising and falling here, onrushing, bursting, and dissolving, have little kinship with waves at sea, with those long bodies of the ocean's pulse. They are shapes of violence and the instancy of creation, towering pyramids crested with a splash of white, rising only to topple upstream as the downcurrent rushes at their base. Lifted for an instant of being into a beauty of pure form and the rising curve, they resemble nothing so much as the decorative and symbolic waves of the artists of Japan.

Enclosing the pool, in a strange contrast of mood,

stands an almost sylvan scene, a country shore of grass and trees and a noontide restfulness of shade.

A bold turn of a gravel promontory, and one escapes out of the caldron into a broading reach of calmer water. Widening, widening to a lake, the river achieves an afternoon peace, and there comes slowly into view a landscape so much part of the old beauty of the past, a landscape so poignantly and profoundly American, that time seems to have stood still awhile above the river.

It is the landscape of Fenimore Cooper and Leatherstocking. Only canoes and bateaux should be using these miles of wide and peaceful water. Another lake has come into being; the Lac St. François; a stretch some twenty-five miles long by some half a dozen wide. Across this placidity of milk, this quiet of a steel engraving, the level shores seem farther away than they really are, and beyond their dreamlike fields and distant, unsubstantial woods blue mountains rise like painted shapes of the older line and mood. Even the few islands in sight are the islands one sees in the older American prints, each one trailing off downstream with a submerged spur from whose tall grasses the redwinged blackbirds rise. All sign and show of industrial perversion has melted from sight. It is the America of Audubon, the country of the *Last of the Mohicans*.

The lake narrowing again to a main stream, a series of almost continuous rapids some fifteen miles in length carry one down their invisible slope in a broad and furious rush. The passage wanders, now racing through open country, now roaring desolately between scrub woods and ragged shores, the separate and thousand torrents mingling and pressing together in one wild and violent skein. The ship winds and turns like a snake searching its way through obstructions in the grass. At the close of the passage the Ottawa enters from the north, bringing down its brownish silt to darken the wider reach ahead.

Another and a smaller lake, and Montreal is in sight, its fogs of smoke melting into one haze with the darkening afternoon. The Lachine is at hand. Once more comes the headlong and universal rush, and a sight of foam breaking and shaking to the distant rims of the river shores. This final fury passed, the vessel crosses to its wharf, having followed the St. Lawrence downhill in a fall of some two hundred and twenty-three feet from the mean summer level of Ontario.

From some crevice of the nearer northern shore, cormorants rise primitive and black, birds of the earth's past, and fly low and in line over the harbor reach, vanishing behind the ships. In the aerial light which follows sunset, that light which is without source and casts no shadows, the river in vast swirls pours onward to the sea.

CHAPTER ONE

Arrival in New France

I CAME to the St. Lawrence from the wilderness frontier of Maine, crossing again the mountains to which one looks from the top of Jackman hill; the day was pleasant and it was late in our northern spring. Beyond the town and a last American glimpse, the road climbed a pass into the forest, winding its way north through walls of trees and old clearings full of the quiet of the woods. Presently after some miles of climbing came the more ragged country of the height of land and, by a scatter of tourist shops and signs, the trivial concrete marker of the line.

Here it is that the road descends, passing one of the great divisions of the continent, and Maine and the republic fall behind together with those streams flowing eastward to the sea. Crossing from an Atlantic slope turned upon the south to one turned upon the north, the traveler has come to a new country, and the light before him is already that of a changed, a colder, and a vaster sky. As he stands facing the mighty northern flowing of the landscape and the great and paler distances of space, the sun is always in the world behind shining with another gleam beyond the height of the frontier. The forest, too, has changed its character. On every side the white pine has given way to the dark masses and tenacities of the more northern spruce, whilst the mountain birch, lover of the north, now towers in new columns above undergrowths of mountain ash and fir. A kind of lumbering which is little more than a sort of ragged gleaning is forever going on here in the forest, and the first houses to be seen are the cabins of the woodsmen by the road.

On the morning of which I write, to one side of a first unpainted shack or house of boards two men were skinning a bear. The poor creature lay extended on an improvised trestle in the sun, a mass of solid, bear-shaped meat emerging from the fur, the skin of a fore-paw hanging to one side. The hunters were two young French-Canadian frontiersmen in their woodsmen's boots and heavy woolen clothes, and as they worked expertly with their knives, each to his side, a little girl came out of the house to watch, standing and staring in the dooryard with a small child's abstracted reverie.

A little beyond this part of the frontier the road descends a hill cleared of higher timber to the west, and there waits a view which makes as dramatic a transition, I think, as any in the world. To the south whence one has come and to the east at one's right hand rises the barrier of the frontier and beyond it the unseen elms of Maine and all the large ease of the American mood; to the west, like a sort of apparition, stands . . . France. Some four or five miles away across the gorge of the mountain stream which is soon to become one with the Chaudière is such a village on a cleared hill as one may see almost anywhere in France itself. Distant and grey, massed in something of a silhouette about its church and lifted against an American and northern sky, the nameless hamlet is symbol as well as place, a first outpost, so to speak, of the ancient and traditional agriculture of Europe with its religious mysteries of life and death and the plough. It is poor, it is frontier, but it is the way of life of another world. Beneath their faintest touch of reviving green these fields remain obstinately American; only a thousand upon a thousand years of rain and the patient hand of man will smooth

these glacial slopes to the noble contours of the Lyonnais or the Île de France. But the task has begun, and day by day the land changes while the contemporary years and their violences and shapes pass like the shadows of clouds upon it and are gone.

Here and there, in farm country beyond, great springtide piles of brush were burning, the smoke rolling off towards the seasonal rush of the Chaudière, and at a first great field there was going on a venturesome and muddy ploughing. A high wind of spring roared across the land, shaking the boughs of trees just coming into leaf, and blowing away the last of the long cold winter of the north. When the fields had grown warm, in would go the white-flowering buckwheat and the oats, the household patch of tobacco, the kitchen garden with its pride of lettuces, and the possible small field of Indian corn.

There is nothing like following a river to put one into the traveler's frame of mind, and the Chaudière is a good companion. Holding to the road for miles it changes, as one descends, from a mountain rapid to a wide and civil stream. The landscape is now a great cleared valley with hills to each side separated by the river and a floor of meadow lowland; the wilderness (more woodlot than wilderness) standing with the left-overness of old snow here and there on farthest heights. Now come towns, the first of the small, picturesque brick and wooden towns of Lower Canada with their small French houses standing sociably side by side along one greater street, maples or poplars in a row, and English sparrows talkative in the leaves. It was pleasant to stop awhile at the entrance to such a place and enjoy the new country, the road, the river, and the sun. On the open slopes across the flowing of the stream were farms and barns, and a road below and a road above, as in the song, whilst behind, coming and going past the poplar trunks, went the butcher, the baker, and the candlestick maker, each with his lettered cart and good, well-fed comfortable horse. It was by these very roads, I thought, that Arnold's men marched to Quebec, hav-

ing emerged from the frontier like so many hairy and
tattered Ishmaels of the woods. Here, by the stream,
under this different light, were the settlements whose
people were so kind: it was at these doors that they
came knocking in the cold of sunrise or in the first dark
of a November night to have hot bowls of soup thrust
into their hands and great morsels of the good, life-
giving habitant bread. The people in their farms and
villages were friendly to the Americans and their venture, wishing them success, but their leaders would have
none of it, and kept their little nation faithful to the
still new and alien crown.

Some twenty miles south of Quebec the Chaudière,
inclining west, vanished away valley and all, and I
found myself upon the tableland whose unseen bound
is the great St. Lawrence gorge. It was landscape now
such as one might encounter in New England, a level
of dark scrub thickets rooted in swamps and with clearings fenced between; and the houses, I noticed, had
many of them fallen away from any French tradition,
being but modern boxes standing in the fields. Behind
a fence, and somewhat by itself, a great Calvaire lifted
its ancient drama to the road, the cross and the lament-
ing figures bright with a light that hardly yet was
warmth, and turned in immobility against the west and
the hurrying bluster of the day. Then the Laurentians
rose, low shapes of blue in the north, bounds of the
white man's eastern North America. The plough has not
passed that uninhabited and solitary wall, there is no
smoke of hearths in that wide air.

It was the old city I saw first, even as I remembered
and expected, the modern buildings of the upper town

coming into view across the last few miles of the plateau. The top of Quebec rock is a little higher than the plateau to this side, and it is clear that the town overhangs a gulf, but the deep and sudden gorge waits to reveal itself, and the river moves hidden below. It was another story when I descended the steeps of Levis down into the gorge, and reached the familiar ferry, making my way aboard in a modern noise and roar of trucks, a din of bilingual shouts and orders, and the harsh departing grind of gangway chains. It was the spring, the great river was muddy and high with inland waters, and beneath the wind and brownish pyramids of waves the force of a continent flowed in currents that seized upon the keel and passed the side in boilings and in streams of muddy glass. Beyond the city, in the widening bay between the Isle of Orleans and the rock, a ground swell labored that might have been the last of some easterly at sea, but was more surely a part of the day's struggle of the swollen river and the tide. Here, at the inland gate of the inland continent, was the rediscovered sea; here, almost a thousand miles from the light of Belle Isle, was the tide now meeting in battle, now joining in one vast and outward strength the waters of Niagara.

The great rock of Quebec towered above, inconceivably grey and old, a fragment of archaic North America and the forest with the great river rushing in seasonal violence by its side. In such fissures and clefts of the naked stone as grass could find a lodging, there were already streaks and lines of springtime green; above were the beautiful and austere walls of the great fortifications merging to the right with the steeples and towers of the town. What a long conflict of men and nations, of rival ambitions, hopes, and ways of life had taken place above these waters! What heroisms and endurances had been a part of the long defense, and what a pageantry of arms and ships of war a part of the unyielding perseverance of attack! The great river had been a part of the historic drama, now leading the enemy to the very foot of the rock, now destroying him in the night and storm and covering its wild shores with the wreckage of his ships and the red-coated bodies of his dead. Then had come a last and desperate summer, an August hazy with the smoke of a burning country-side, and a September morning with a sudden unexpected sound of battle from the west of the city and the heights. When the last of the volleys and the heavier rolling of artillery had died away, the inland of a continent had changed hands, and a new flag had rippled off into the wind.

All this had taken place scarce two hundred years ago. What had happened the while to the new masters and the old, to people and to ways of life, and to this great North American scene? Vast as nature and unconcerned with the lives and violences of men, the St. Lawrence rushed from its gorge eastward through the spring and the day, widening at the spur of Quebec rock into the valley which breaks a continent apart. To the side of the mountain roads in the Laurentians there would still be old snow, blackened and crystallized to ice beneath the dark of trees: in the old city above, the mood of winter and isolation would have yielded to the opening of the stream. The ferry reached the bank and let us all off in another din of engines, and I made my way out of it up into the town.

CHAPTER TWO

The City on the Rock

I

As one stands on the height of Dufferin Terrace looking eastward down the river, it is the tremendous scale of the landscape ahead which immediately arrests the eye. It is a panorama of distant mountains and great shores, faraway skies, and a river mighty as ocean in a path, and there is nothing in the scene to be measured by the familiar either in Europe or the coastal east of America. What stands so vast is something powerful and new, a first revelation in the north of the huge, archaic, and formidable continent dividing whole oceans with its shores. Not western in its look (that revelation comes by the levels of Lac St. Pierre) it is entirely western in space and measure. This earth is not France or England or even New England or Virginia. It is alien to Europe and to memories of Europe. It is the buffalo and the plain, the rattlesnake coiled on the prairie, and the green pillars of the corn.

Looking eastward to this continental scene the city stands as on the prow of a ship of earth and rock, the turbid rush of the narrows to one side, the St. Charles tributary to the other. Below the historic southern cliff a rim of lowland borders the greater stream, turning the prow to meet with the industrialized banks of the St. Charles; on these levels stands the lower town. It is a place of business now, carried on in rather grim buildings of the gaslit age, a town of wharves, narrow streets, small factories, filling stations, and stores with bright paint and dirty windows. The commercialism is more British in core than French, but an exported Americanism is making the exterior its own. On the St. Lawrence side, going westward along the cliff, what is left of the old French and shipping quarter takes form in the general huddle; it is the old quarter of "sous 'le 'cap." Champlain's own house, the fur trade warehouses, and the first settlement stood somewhere here, backed up against the rock. Indeed, his votive church still stands, transformed by several complete fires yet somehow or other managing emotionally to persevere. One wanders by Norman roofs with Norman gables and Norman chimneys, relics of a past when human beings would seem to have come into the world with a sense of beauty as naturally as they arrived with a right hand. There is a square, too, which I visit for it is very French and provincial still with its cobblestones, French windows, and lace curtains with elegant waists; and very Quebec with the dusty cliff of the citadel rising close behind. Who, as a child, having pressed a nose against the harsh machine thread of such a curtain ever can forget its grey smell of the quintessence of all dust? The English sparrows know the place, whirring up from underfoot, and sea gulls rise and sail with searching eyes over the wharves and the near rush and streaming of the river.

But it is the upper town, the region atop the cliff, which gives one the genuine and little appreciated key to the spirit of the place. In a way, it is a key to much one encounters in French Canada. Passing these old

houses, these windows filled with books, religious manuals, and objects of Catholic devotion, it comes upon
me again that this city has little to do with either the
seventeenth or the eighteenth century, but everything
to do with a particularly characteristic and romantically
complete period of the nineteenth. Of the seventeenth
century, little remains. The old rooms and old wards of
the Hôpital Saint Louis, built by Bishop Saint-Vallier,
are the most touching of the survivals. Of the eighteenth, there stands the fine wing of the Grand Sémi-
naire and the little chapel there of Monseigneur Briand;
there are also a few houses. (Of the Ursuline Chapel,
more anon.) The ancien régime has melted like the
snow. The clock of architectural time on the rock
stands at the mood of 1830. What the core of old
Quebec really recalls, under its modernity and its guide-
books, is a French provincial town of the time of Louis
Philippe which has managed to get itself enclosed in a
British military wall. What has been added of earliest
Victorian England has merely strengthened the effect.
These older streets with their grim façades and serious
doorways are not backgrounds for eighteenth century
wigs and brocades. They are meant to frame groups of
such handsome young women in hooded bonnets and
uglily-quaint puffed sleeves as one sees in the portraits
of Ingres or might read of in Balzac. Respectable gentlemen, fathers of families, merchants and bankers, should
be behind these panes, all looking a little like M. de
Lamartine. I think of them going to Sunday mass on
an April morning, passing first even such a young man
as might be a colonial Lucien de Rubempré and then a
band of Hurons from Lorette in their Sunday gala of

broadcloth and beadwork finery—all to a sound of French and Catholic bells brought up the river long ago when the ice melted in some forgotten spring.

There is little of what the French call *riant* about Quebec. It is a place forte in character as well as in natural appearance, a kind of fortress of the courage and tenacity of man facing on the one hand the intermittent human enemy and on the other the timeless weight of nature and the sure, recurrent savagery of winter and the cold. People come and go with their beliefs and fancies, but stone and shadow and the corner of the street remember and remain. There is memory in these walls, a timeless thought of the sound of other drums, of the white of another flag stirring its gold lilies in this huge and wilderness air. Modernity means little to this spirit. It does not see or hear, it reflects. The floes which all winter long have washed to and fro dissolve in the warming air, the snow melts from the rock, and from a savagery of white the great stream turns to its annual moment of bright and beautiful blue. In the eternal recurrence, on a frontier of nature, the spirit here is a force and strong awareness. Not without poetic wisdom has the following motto been chosen for the heraldic escutcheon of the city: "Je me souviens" ("I remember").

II

As I wander about Quebec this pleasant morning after rain, it is of the clergy I think first, for this is much their city. No street seems to be without its ecclesiastical figures; everywhere they come and go in soft hats and shovel hats, black coats and black capes and "the wind in their gowns." Nuns, too, are passing in the sunlight in their decorum of black, and every now and then strides by, with younger step, one of the teaching brothers who wear the broad French hat, the French eighteenth century soutane, and the white neck cloth of the abbés of old France. Habits and gowns, orders and brotherhoods, metropolitan dignities and parish simplicities, no part of the picture of Quebec is more native to the canvas than this sense and awareness of the church. For the historian it is something unique in the world, a glimpse of eighteenth century French Catholicism such as he may find it in a thousand old books and prints with its convents and great establishments, its gardens and schools, in the heart of the eighteenth century cities. Only here no French Revolution has thundered over its roofs and beaten at its doors; no clubs of Jacobins, Cordeliers or Feuillants have stamped and shouted in its dispossessed monasteries, a schismatic Lion having held the river for the Lilies and the Cross.

There was a strong missionary spirit to seventeenth century Catholicism. It was an age in which religion had put on the outward trappings of the world, filling her churches with Italianate theatricality, wooden marble, and angels in Roman armor, all twiddly nonsense to us now, but behind this façade, the timeless spirit of devotion burned with a clear flame. In country houses of France, pious ladies read books of praise or mystical philosophy and corresponded with other ladies of their mind, tireless and heroic evangelists prepared for martyrdom, and ships and the cross sailed all the seven seas. One went directly from an artificial tapestry of courts and formidable wigs to the wilderness in its elemental savagery, and to death in some most torturing and repulsive form. It is to be noted that the men and women who went forth to such ordeals were not adventurers, but people of quiet and of books, men and women used to gardens and meditation, to the peace of enclosing walls and the summer sound of leaves. Surely no more poignant testimony to the courage and endurance possible to the human spirit exists greater than these lives.

The foundations of the Ursuline community at Quebec is a work of this spirit and this age. Two heroic women, the Venerable Mère Marie de l'Incarnation and a young and pious widow, Madame Madeleine de Chauvigny de la Peltrie, were its founders, arriving in Canada in 1639. (Champlain had died in 1635.) Their allotment of land on the rock once cleared, and a shelter built, the little community began the task for which it had crossed the seas—the conversion and education of the daughters of the forest. Little Montagnais girls with their birchbark coffers and sealskin belts, Hurons with their deerskin bags, and petites Iroquoises were got together to be taught prayers and convent needlework, and to hear the psalms read by hearthlight and candlelight. On the whole, alas, the petites Montagnaises, Huronnes, Algonkuines, and Iroquoises didn't give a hang. Their brown eyes remained full of the shadows of the forest, they were not moved by the redemptive mysteries of Israel. One after another, maidens who had been expected to give some propriety to the Stone Age in the spruces—or become nuns—went wild as fawns. These simple creatures, it appeared, wished to get married. Still the Ursulines persevered. With one particular pupil they achieved so great a success that her name has come down to us; the good, the pious Thérèse la Huronne who ended her days in the odor of sanctity. Meanwhile the French community was growing and the Indians were falling back. Presently the "seminaire sauvage" was closed and the "pensionnat Français" made the center of the work.

Three hundred years have passed over Quebec and the river since the first garden and the first chapel of the Ursulines were made upon the rock. The Indian and the fur trader have become a part of legend and the past, the ships of France are no more, and a new flag flies over the snow, but still the same garden waits for the late Canadian spring; still rises "like a fountain night and day" the murmur of prayer. Sharing every adventure, every triumph and vicissitude of the colony, the Ursuline community has become something more than a part of Canadian history; it is a part of the very soul of old French Canada. Whatever politics and wars might have accomplished, here by this garden and these walls was continuity. Today, where wounded and dying men of the great battle were laid on their beds of straw and green Canadian boughs—a part of the buildings having been commandeered—and hard by where Montcalm sleeps beneath the chapel wall, little girls still learn their lessons, their young voices coming birdlike through some window open to the spring. "La Lecture et l'Écriture, la Grammaire, la Littérature et la Composition, l'Histoire Sacrée et l'Histoire Profane, la Géographie et la Cosmographie"—they can have them all. Being under cloistered rule, the sisters are seldom seen. Their whole lives are led in the shelter of their walls and their hidden garden, whose paths they walk in their distinguished black and white.

Were I to be asked where in Quebec (and I might add in all of Canada) the mood of the old royalist adventure of New France was most poignantly to be felt, where the visible symbols of its being were best to be seen in their withdrawn authority, I should answer the chapel of the Ursulines. The chapel is not old, being the fourth to occupy the historic site, but so entirely simple is the modern masonry that the architectural effect is essentially timeless, and the altar and the furniture are those of previous chapels of the seventeenth and eighteenth centuries. The altar is classical France and eighteenth century Catholicism, a great affair of gilt and pillars.

No noise intrudes. There is peace and beauty, and the little strangeness of many candle flames. To the right of the altar, an arch with a grille stands in the wall dividing the chapel and the outer world from the conventional enclosure to one side where the nuns come quietly to pray. When I last visited the chapel, it was in the later morning. Mass had been said and a smoke of incense lingered in the small and churchly quiet; in the pews, two or three women of the laity remained in prayer. Behind the grille, kneeling in the other room, in her other world, a solitary religieuse continued her own meditation, coiffed head inclined above her hands. The lilies and the crown, the adventure of the river, the sword, and the cross were contained in the space as in a reliquary, with the ancient altar and its lights enclosed in a remembering peace.

III

The industrial age has so covered the face of the earth with negative dirt, with wreckage, pollution, and yahoo squalor, that I find it a relief now and then to discover myself in dirt of a positive kind. By positive dirt, I mean such dirt as one may find about an open market place, even such dirt which has something to do with living. Old cabbage leaves underfoot, oats spit over paving stones by some vacant-minded horse lifting his head a moment from his pail, a half-eaten apple in a gutter in the sun—all these are the earth's own debris. There is no horror to them as there is to a brook clogged with rags and filth. Indeed, there is something about an open-air market which stirs and reassures the honest animality in human character.

The surface of any city, for all the sun-glints on the automobiles, for all the wires, the brick, motion, and noise, has but a borrowed and a robot life; abstract as a mathematical formula, it exists only when people have it in their minds. But turn a corner to the market, and there again are beginnings, and once again the earth and life and death.

There are two markets in Quebec, one in the old square I have mentioned as "sous le cap" and the other down the hill to the west in a street near the manufacturing world of the St. Charles. It is to this second market that I most often go, crossing an industrial ugliness which has bloated itself downhill, and emerging into a morning's oasis of country things and country faces. Life then seems to me to have again an earth reality. The stalls are the merest temporizations, a board across two boxes or even a basket and a chair, but everything is piled high, is fresh and green, is country-vigorous; leaves, cheeses, honeycombs, chickens, legs of lamb, maple syrup and blood puddings. Huge, Gothic stalks of rhubarb are everywhere, the archvegetable of French Canada. Crisp, sourish-sweet, living, and inwardly green, it is the first thing in the spring to break from the thawing soil. The faces are country faces, shrewd and out-of-doorish, reflecting the business mood of the morning: one must not waste their time, now that they have come in from their farms and their account books, and from their traffic of life and death.

It is not, however, these maple sugar and rhubarb people I go to see. I go to find my own people, the market herbalists, the good traditionalists who keep alive the old wisdom of the North American forest, remembering the virtues of its native roots and leaves. Their stalls are humble, a board on a barrel top sometimes, and their stock in trade is scarcely more than a great paper bag full of little bundles of roots, leaves, and barks spread patiently on a plank in the cold morning sun. Now and then a bottle or two makes its appearance, a decoction of goldenrod, perhaps, or a tonic of bitter thoroughwort. These bottled remedies are often perilous-looking stuff, muddy and milky at once, and with a pinkish tint suggestive of a red shirt having been washed in the concoction. But here are dry, earthy roots of the wild angelica, "la belle angélique, monsieur," which make a brew good for the digestion and the general health; here a fine, forest-scented bundle of fresh spruce bark for ailing kidneys, here a little phial of the clear and golden pitch of the fir balsam, the native Algon-

quin remedy for frostbites and sores. How many an
American captive, on the long and tragic trail to Canada, has had this smeared on frozen toes and hands! On
these stalls the Indian pharmacopoeia blends with the
seventeenth century wisdom of peasant France, native

gold thread and the introduced weed both helping
Aesculapius. But it is always the forest which seems to
stand in greater authority.

The keeper of such a stall is usually some pleasant
older woman dressed in country black, and sitting alone
behind her roots and leaves. She has brought her knit-
ting; the grey wool shakes and the needles twist, and out
of the corner of her eye she watches the housewives of
Quebec passing by with their baskets and their greens.
Sometimes a tall, Indian-looking man arrives, with a

taciturn little son, and there is often a young and friendly fellow in country clothes patched and mended to the last homespun seam. My herbalists take life more easily than the farmers. They are more ready to talk and are glad to discuss the virtues of their plants. I always buy various things, which are given to me rolled in a scrap of newspaper. Five cents, ten cents, prices are low, but the little transaction is always given a human dignity with its habitant good manners. "Merci, monsieur," "Merci, madame," and away I go with pockets as mysterious and fragrant as an Indian medicine man's.

There are times when we have long Wife-of-Bath-ish colloquies about our human ills. These human ills, I fear, do not weigh very heavily upon my mind. What touches me when I go among the herbsellers is a sense of life, of something old and deeply rooted which has lived on into our own years, careless of the dull education slapped on everybody like a grey paint, something whose life is not of books, but of the old wisdom, of the sense of wonder, and the earth.

IV

Modern Quebec in terms of its people is never more at its best than on summer evenings when the whole town goes to walk on Dufferin Terrace. Here high above the river and the roofs of the lower town, strolling as it were in mid-air and the evening haze with the vast hotel looming mountainous behind, a comfortably uncrowded crowd walks in social promenade on the old comfortable boards. One stream moves towards the military slopes of the citadel, another towards the statue of Champlain, both streams turning and returning at the ends of the promenade, the dusk meanwhile deepening. It is rather like a Spanish "paseo" though less formal in its paths of walking, and I imagine that it is perhaps the only thing of its kind to be found north of Spanish America. The spectacle is not colorful as I have seen it in Salamanca, for the clothes are the dark commonplaces of the industrial north, but it has a profound and debonair humanity, and it is cheerful to become a part of its contented and sociable rhythm. Pleasant customs in a civilization are singularly dependent upon public good manners: some sort of convention must exist, and the terrace has from the first agreed with a particularly Catholic and Latin acquiescence. It is unfailingly well-behaved, taking its stroll like an easy and civilized pleasure; one is gratefully spared the lout on a lark. Girls walk by twos and threes even as they would in Spain; families pass at the family gait, elderly couples stroll together, the young men walk and talk, and solitaries watch from comfortable benches. Most of the conversation is in French though now and then one hears the business accent of the English tongue. To wear a straw hat is to announce oneself as a visiting American.

A sudden and somewhat unplaced crash and the sunset gun fires from the great rock of the citadel. Twilight deepens in the gorge below, brightening the lights of the ferries, and a last cold gleam dies from the vast sky eastward above the river. The families are going home; the children must be put to bed. A little more strolling by electric light, and the rest of Quebec will be following after them, the quiet murmur of the passing feet and the decorum of the voices withdrawing out of an early night grown cold and too hazy above for any star.

CHAPTER THREE

The American Captives

I

GREAT aspects of nature such as a fine land-scape or an evening gathering of cloud are slow to reveal themselves. The immediate glimpse which seemed at first so complete is but a moment in the great and continuous flowing which is the being of all things: within the fragment of time are moving all the innumerable forces of the world. The vast rhythms of nature and the earth, the august and processional seasons, the annual drama of the sun together with a thousand upon a thousand mysteries of pure caprice and fantasy, these are a part of the surface of a stone. With the passing of a shadow from a great and distant mountain, with the fall of some single last and resplendent leaf, we inhabit another world. The bodiless wind of summer is a rush across the earth, a shaking of trees and a flowing upon the grass; in winter it is a river revealed in falling snow, a torrent eddying and streaming over field and ocean to some final quiet of the sky. Even thus the intricacy and splendor of any great aspect wait upon time for revela-tion, only with time and the human spirit coming to a full significance.

In all nature there is nothing slower to reveal itself than the intricate being of a forest. Fixed in the earth, a part of the established landscape like a solitary moun-

tain or an arm of the sea, and like them subject to the
will of the year, it is also a part of life, sharing with the
creatures who keep to its shadows the ambitions and the
hazards of sentient existence. Like a multitude, it is a
collective being, a natural presence with its own
frontiers, its own laws, and its own green mystery and
power; like a multitude again, it is a standing-together-
ness of individuals, each with its own nature, its or-
dained desires, and its response to the caprice of the
world in which it lives. Fixed yet alive, a thing in itself
yet many things, the forest is simple only in its greater
manifestations. Its subtleties are as numberless as its
leaves. While one region will be loud with the roar of
wind, another will unaccountably be still as a cave: the
snow on one path will fall with all the fury of a storm;
on another, sift through unstirring branches gentle and
noiseless as a kind of cosmic dust. A place of life and the
thrust of life, of rivalries and long endurances together
with a multitudinous wooden sluggishness of dying,
long outliving men and even nations, the forest keeps
its counsel, opening to no human key of awareness its
monstrous secrecies.

If the splendor of the southern forest comes with
new leaves and the poignancy of spring, it is with the
austere winter that the northern evergreen forest comes
into its own. Lovely as the autumn may be with its
hardwoods standing like pillars of gold among the
towers of the pines, all in the brighter and clearer air—
the winter with its fierceness of light and universal
pageantry of white and green is the true climax of the
year. What has been lost is as nothing compared to
beauty and mystery, the fantasy and miracle arriving

with the snow. Against the universal white which has
covered all the earth, trees rise everywhere in sharper
and more individual presence, their evergreen forms, so
stable in summer, altered with the weight of snow to
drooping curves and sagging arabesques. The forest is
far more still in winter than it is in summer, and a
bird's call may be a small adventure in its loneliness.
Under the direct and savage sky a new dignity, a new
authority, encloses the very being of the wood. After a
great storm when the moon nears the full and the
northern lights chance to appear you shall come upon
no greater strangeness of beauty in all nature than the
forest standing in its silences of moonlight laden and
robed with the motionless garlands of the snow.

Wave upon wave of green, an unknown wilderness,
the great aboriginal forest of the American northeast
swept from New England north to the St. Lawrence,
and crossing the river, died away beyond the height of
land in the arctic barrens and the cold. Archaic and
confused beyond any European measure, a scene of
savagery and savage forces both present and anciently
vanished away, the forest rolled on over its mountains to its own empty and unhuman sky, closing the
vista with the pallor and defiance of the north. In the
seaward valley of the river and more particularly to its
farther shore, the forest was much as it is today, a
growth of spruce, hemlock, and tamarack—the colder
evergreens—with white birches for their company, and
a scattering of "popples," maples, and other hardwoods
between. The white pine grew, but was not really at
home among its brethren. Its region lay to the south and
south again beyond the mountain shapes of the debat-

able frontier. There, in the wilderness whose streams found their way to the Atlantic, stood the greater trees, the white pines grown to columns tall as masts and as straight, the hemlock likewise huger grown, the maples and the oaks, the American forest beech with its rounded top and muscled roundness of branch. The region had its own nobility. Only men of the Stone Age knew its trails and portages: on the shores of its ponds the white man's foot had not trodden out the delicate impression of the moccasin.

Back and forth across the seasons went the birds, the parti-colored ducks following the bright, solitary lakes; in the shallows the moose lifted his grotesque head chewing on the lily root he had nuzzled from the mud. Collecting and centering the mood Katahdin rose, the sacred mountain untouched of human feet; Katahdin, the forest Sinai of the Abenakis on whose blue slopes of terror dwelt the gods.

Who were the first Americans to penetrate this solitude between the river of New France and the English on the coast? Who first saw the great sea of the forest and the nameless lakes flowing with whitecaps like a seeming river under the burly of some blue October wind? Not the blackrobe missionary and the fur trader of New France, those two earliest explorers of inland America, for they were busy following the St. Lawrence to the west. With promising country ahead and great Indian nations waiting for the gospel and the mass, adventurings toward the mountain barrier were at first of minor importance. Yet even in these earliest days white men and women and little children had crossed the entire wilderness. With their Indian captors,

the painted and terrifying "tawnies," they had walked
its overshadowed trails, their Puritan brogues falling to
pieces on the wilderness rocks, their Puritan clothes
tearing on many an unfriendly branch. Perhaps in all
American history there is nothing more poignant and
moving than the lives of these colonial prisoners carried off to Canada in the old French wars. For some the
passage through the forest remained only a dark memory, a confused record of travel afoot and by canoe, of
campfires, savagery, and the animal hunger for one's
daily fragment of singed meat. For others the forest
remained a power which kept them henceforth for its
own. Mehitables and Marys, Samuels, Thomases, and
Jonathans—to what strange and hybrid destinies they
marched along the rivers and beneath the overhead
murmur of the trees! Of the three captives whose stories
I set down, one turned to France and religion; one obstinately remained an Indian; whilst the last remained an
habitant Yankee, making his final and poignant choice
as the boat sent to fetch him left the shore.

II

The War of the Spanish Succession, which began
in the great apartments at Versailles, was not long in
reaching the granite ledges of the New England coast.
With hostile Indians and the paths of the forest at their
backs, and French Canada at the end of those paths, the
frontier settlements of the coast of Maine stood in particular peril of destruction.

On August 10, 1703, at nine o'clock of a pleasant
summer's morning, a band of French and Indians made

a surprise attack on the village of Wells. Painted like devils from some aboriginal hell and sounding that strange Indian ululation of war, that clear, birdlike piping which has the terror of the nonhuman, the Abenakis went swiftly to their looting and killing. Soon many of the houses were in flames. When the attack slackened, some thirty-nine of the inhabitants had either been killed or captured. The Indians then gathered their prisoners together, the men, women and little children standing to one side in their forlornness and anxiety, and turning them from the smoke and the August sea, marched them off into the unknown country of the woods.

The village, making a list of the missing, presently discovered that a little girl of seven had been carried away by the raiders. This was Esther Wheelwright, daughter of John and Mary Wheelwright, and granddaughter of the Puritan minister who, with his friends, had founded the town. One sees her as a child of the frontier yeomanry moving against the background of some great colonial hearth with its blackened pots and wooden spoons, its birchbark containers and its English knives. Two years pass, and a letter from an American prisoner in Quebec brings news that some of the captives from Wells are in the city. Esther was not mentioned. Where, then, was she? Had so small a person died somewhere on the long march through the wilderness? More years passed, and there was still no news from Canada. Esther was not in New France. For some reason or other her Indian captor (whose personal property she happened to be) had not sold her to the French, but kept her in an Indian village in the wilderness of the upper Kennebec. For six years she had lived as an Indian, wearing the rags and tatters of their clothes and speaking their tongue. It was in this situation that she was discovered by a kindly and pious missionary priest, Father Bigot, and was by him ultimately ransomed from her captors.

Then came a great and surprising change. Arriving on the St. Lawrence, the little "Englishwoman" was given over to the hospitable care of two great personages, de Vaudreuil, the governor of New France, and his lady. From the forest and the primitive noise and dirt of an Abenaki village, Esther Wheelwright passed to the French decency and order of the governor's own house. She was then a girl of twelve or thirteen. On January 18, 1709, Mme. de Vaudreuil brought the child to the Ursulines. "Madame La Marquise brought us a little anglaise as a pupil," says the register. The New England connection, it would seem, had become somewhat nebulous, though it was to assert itself later and be touchingly and dutifully respected.

Far away in New England, John and Mary Wheelwright had been having other children. Including Esther, there had been eleven altogether. Under the care of the Ursulines, some deep religious sense woke in the child, and she accepted Catholicism with fervor and fell easily into the French way of life. Yet de Vaudreuil would not allow her to take the first steps of her profession as a nun. Not till October 2, 1712, after two years of complicated negotiations concerning all prisoners, years in which Esther does not seem to figure, did Father Bigot's protégée begin her novitiate at the Ursulines' of Quebec. The old priest insisted on paying all the expenses of the ceremony. "Thy hand shall lead me and thy right hand shall hold me" was his text.

That Esther's family knew where she was is clear. A note in the original records of the Ursuline community states that following the girl's profession as a nun her family in New England were notified, and that they responded lovingly "with letters and gifts."

She was now la Sœur Esther Marie Joseph de l'Enfant Jésus. In the convent above the St. Lawrence the placid and ordered life of a French religieuse gathered a Puritan into its ancient routine of teaching and prayer. The long years and the long winters passed over the rock. In January, 1754, when Sœur Esther was in her fifty-eighth year, a young man who had come up from Boston through the Maine woods most unexpectedly presented himself at the convent door. It was a colonial officer, Major Nathaniel Wheelwright, her brother's son, and he had arrived in Quebec to discuss an exchange of prisoners taken in the frontier skirmishes which had been fought in America during the years of nominal European peace. The young man gave his kinswoman—"my Aunt Esther Wheelwright"—a miniature of her mother painted as a young woman, and presented to the Ursuline community "a silver flagon, some fine linen, and a silver knife and fork and spoon."

Then came the siege and its bombardments, its fires and destructions, the final battle on the heights and the death of Montcalm. At the beginning of hostilities —the Ursuline convent being very exposed to cannon fire—the community of nuns had taken refuge at the Hôpital Général. Eight sisters, however, remained at the convent itself to take what care they could of their endangered home. Their quarters were in the great cellars of the buildings and they could hear through the rock the detonation of the shells. Sœur Esther Marie, then a woman of sixty-seven, was one of this group. In the terrible silence which lay upon the city after the defeat upon the plains, the body of Montcalm was brought at night from the house of the surgeon Arnoux to the chapel of the Ursulines. There, by candlelight, amid the sound of Latin and while all wept, they buried him in an opening of the foundations an enemy shell had pierced beneath the wall. Holding their tapers, the sisters stood to one side, their dark habits massed in somber contrast to the bright colors of the military attendance, while unseen and unheard the great river seemingly carried away in the night the last fragment of the national and religious dream.

In December, 1760, three months after the capitulation at Montreal, Sœur Esther Marie was elected superior of the Ursulines of Quebec. The anxiety, poverty and distress which shadowed all French Canada had not spared the community. Moreover, its buildings were in ruin. Wherever a chimney was still usable and a roof intact the sisters gathered together. Finding that the British officers had a fancy for the French and Indian handicraft of embroidery on birchbark, they kept busily at their needles, embroidering card cases and birch whatnots for the young, half-frozen subalterns. The community was desperately poor, and the life of the entire colony tragically disorganized. As a leader of the French, it was more than once the new superior's duty to discuss matters of policy with Sir John Murray, their new British governor. The spirit of history, were it present, must have thought it a strange and ironic meeting. On the one side stood the venerated abbess, an "anglaise" by blood, granddaughter of that bold and combative Puritan, the Reverend John Wheelwright of the Lincolnshire fens and the wild New England coast; on the other stood Murray in his general's uniform, a Scottish younger son from a castle near Dranmore. There is something very likable about Murray. His letters reveal a nature essentially understanding and kind; as far as he could be he was a friend as well as a conqueror, and he dared much to protect the French from the commercial "harpies and bullies"—the phrase is his— who came settling out of the air to exploit the new prey. The world into whose colonial echoes Esther Wheelwright had been born, the British community with its redcoat values and stanch Protestantism, that society which lives for us in Hogarth and the incomparable "conversation pieces" of Zoffany, had conquered the world into which a caprice of history had led the little child from Wells, and to the service of whose purposes she had dedicated her entire life. Now it was all over, or seemed all over, with the only world she had ever really known. The pomp of Versailles, the great altars and the fluted columns, the august sound of eighteenth century religious song, the white flag with the lilies, and the soldiers with gauntleted and embroidered gloves—all this must have seemed withdrawing like music into a sadness of distance far from her undaunted New England head. Flags, she may have thought, were but a part of time: she would serve the timeless to the end.

    She died in 1780 at the age of eighty-four. There

is much about her in the annals of the Ursulines, and a number of her letters are in existence. They reveal her as a fine and thoughtful person meeting with wisdom and good-tempered fortitude the disasters of her world. Still in use, but not shown, is the silver flagon her nephew put into her hands in the convent parlor on a Quebec winter morning close upon two hundred years ago. The little miniature of her mother may be seen. It has been retouched, a kind of saint's veil has been arranged about the head, and there is a story, perhaps a legend, that this was done in order that Esther Marie might keep this family picture with its ties and memories of "the world."

The most interesting relic, however, is in New England. It is the portrait of Esther Wheelwright as abbess of the Ursulines. Painted in 1761, it was sent by the abbess to her mother who had lived on to advanced age. Painted in Canada when La Tour was painting in France and Reynolds in England, no portrait could be less of the eighteenth century; in manner and spirit there is not a touch of the contemporary European world. It is a pure seventeenth century canvas, even such a likeness as the first Massachusetts Puritans bequeathed to their descendants to measure them and their times with their obstinate and formidable glance. The dignified, wise and self-reliant visage of the woman of middle age who looks at us out of her Ursuline coif does its own honor to so resolved a heritage. The power is there and the character, but there is no harshness in the firm mouth, no defiance of life and kings in the large eyes and assured and disciplined gaze. In the darkened canvas France and New England meet and are at peace.

III

No primitive people known to history have ever led an existence requiring more stark animal endurance than the more northerly tribes of the eastern forest area. The summer life of these Algonquins was communal, those who could do so moving as a village to the coast or to some open riverside avoiding thus the forest when insect pests were at their worst; but their winter life was as elemental as that of beasts of prey. It was their custom to leave their summer encampments with the first frosts and the earlier bird migrations, return to the woods, and break up into small bands and family groups for the battle with the winter. (There are regions of arctic Canada where the same custom holds today.) Each group then hunted for itself in the snow and cold of the deep woods, killing their prey as they could with their Stone Age weapons, and living out the storms in shelters which were little more than movable dens. Now gorged, now hungry to the bone, sleeping at night in choking smoke while the arctic cold gripped the moon-lit immensity about the family lair, father and old grandfather, mother and newborn child somehow managed till the spring. When the sun began to melt the shining icicles, and the caribou snowshoes sank deeper into flattening and wetter snow, those who had out-fought the season presently came together from the woods.

Abenaki shelter or Mohawk village, the Algonquin

path or the Iroquois, Indian life scarcely seems to have been a tempting existence in the forested northeast. All through the earlier colonial period, however, the historian must face. the curious truth that captive white children who had lived as little Indians were again and again returned with difficulty to their original way of

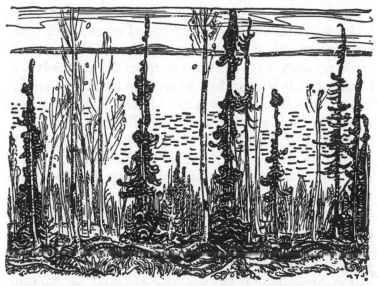

life. When their relatives came at last to ransom them, the children fled like deer into the woods; when they were brought back by force, they escaped at night, rarely to be seen again. Entirely rebellious, they dug in their little Puritan heels and stopped their ears against First and Second Corinthians and the perils of infant damnation. Not for them was the fire on the hearth or the bed in the unfinished chamber with its quilts and straw. They knew something much better. In their noses was the good smell of soft smoke-ripened deer-skin, in their mouths the flavor of game stewed into a porridge with corn, berries, a moose bone, and a palm-ful of maple sugar. Moreover, whether they knew it or not, they were at peace with the tense American earth. The white civilization of their inheritance was at war with the earth; an occupation beginning as a conquest, a clearing, and a killing had fastened on the land with-out a moment's pause of means or mood. The Indians made no such war. They made room for themselves in nature, but it was to their interest to let nature remain what it was. The earth was an ancestral mystery. Across it like the fugitive wind moved the direct and vivid pat-tern of their lives, the hunger and the feasting, the wandering and the hunting, the stoicism of winter and the animal unrest and ecstasy of spring. To disturb the world disturbed the pattern and the ancestral ghosts, and one lived or one died as a part of something no more to be fought than a cloud shadow or a wave in the sea.

The child Eunice Williams had been carried away from the sack of Deerfield when she was between seven and eight years old. She was the daughter of the min-ister of the village and sixth in a family of eleven. In the division of spoil and captives, she fell to the lot of a Mohawk of Caughnawaga, then called St. Louis. (A handful of Iroquois had been induced by missionaries to throw in their fortunes with the French and settle on the river.) The Indian "master" seems to have been very tender with the child. The little girl had need of it, for she had known horror. Her father and mother, taken captive in the same foray of 1704 had come to a tragic parting on the forest path to Montreal, her mother having been tomahawked and killed for her weakness on the trail, leaving her father to continue on to Canada. Later in the year father and daughter met on two occasions; he says the child wished to return, but was not allowed to do so. The final decision in these cases of ransom lay with the Indian captor, and both the Mohawk and the missionaries at the village were unwilling to part with the "pritty" and pleasant child. So whilst her father returned to Massachusetts, Eunice remained at Caughnawaga with the praying Iroquois.

So began a conflict of loyalties and wills which was to last for many years. The years began to pass. There was news now and then of "Mr. Williams' daughter," but no Eunice returned to what the French called "Deerfiel'." "She is in good health," says one informant, "but seemes unwilling to returne." This was in 1707. In 1711 an Abenaki squaw whose two children had been taken by the English was told that she might have them back if she could manage the return of Eunice Williams from Caughnawaga. The woman went faithfully to Montreal, but met with no success. The French governor could not "prevail with the Mohawks for Eunice Williams," but very decently sent home "four English persons" in exchange for the Abenaki children. Then in 1712 and 1713 Colonel Peter Schuyler of Albany took a hand in the affair. Arriving in Montreal on April 15, 1713, he went to the Iroquois settlement to urge Eunice to return to New England at "the instant and earnest desire of her father." He found her rechristened "Margaret" and married to a young Iroquois brave. She appeared, he says, "bashfull in the face but harder than steel in her breast." As she did not seem to understand (or not wish to understand, perhaps) the English tongue, recourse was had to the village priest and the Indian interpreter. All seem to have faithfully translated Schuyler's plea and urged her towards New England, but the young wife only stood silent, continuing "impersuadable to speak." Only after long solicitations, fair offers and earnest requests did she talk. "Zaghte oghte," she said, "it may not be." "And these words were all we could gett from her in almost two hours' time that we talked with her."

Her father tried once more, and then all efforts came to an end. An Indian she preferred to be and an Indian she was to remain. Caughnawaga with its trophies of war, its dust, its hungry Indian dogs, and its furs pegged to the wall was to be her home, and not the broad street of Deerfield and the manse. During her long life of ninety years, however, she thrice made her way back to Deerfield with her husband, Amrusus, and her tawny sons and daughters. The Indians camped in the old orchard of the parsonage; the parson himself having long been gathered to his fathers. Her brothers and sisters of New England visited their sister in her tent. Half-brother Stephen Williams, the minister, used his best arguments with Eunice "to persuade her to tarry and to come and to dwell with us . . ." but his words, like words uttered long, long before were "ineffectual." So he bade Eunice and a daughter farewell "in the parlor" and both "shed tears and were much affected." Next day there would be no smoke rising from a corner of the field.

The Indian path had its own gods; it was strong

medicine. Those who had followed it, and were later returned to their own white inheritance, often heard the shaking of the Indian rattle and the voices of Indian ghosts. I remember the man from Wells who all his life long sat on the floor like an Indian and maintained that they were "better people than the whites." To no other captive, however, does the imagination wander with more feeling than to the "pritty" child of Caughna-waga standing a grown woman with her dark children about her, and watching from her father's orchard the lights of the parsonage appearing in the dusk.

IV

The last story is soon told. It does not aim to present the small canvas of a life, but merely to set down the intense and poignant moment on which a whole life and many other lives depended.

Like Esther Wheelwright, a number of the children taken captive spent their lives among the French. These were children whom the French themselves had redeemed, paying over French money and trade goods in the noisy, caterwauling Indian towns; children, for the most part, whose relatives had been killed or lost sight of in the confusion of the wars. All up and down the river, in the kitchens with the double walls prepared against the cold, small boys and girls exchanged their Old Testament names for the easier names of the Roman saints and forgot their English by the great Canadian hearths. Coming of age, these children commonly married in the French community, the boys founding French families with English surnames, many of which have continued to this day. Misspelled, Frenchified, a puzzle to parish priest and to students of the registers, the English patronymic mingle with the Gallic on the yellowing page, touching the heart with a thought of "battles long ago."

In one of the villages of the river there was a young man of the colonies who had been brought up as a Frenchman and had married a French girl. His uncle on the other side of the frontier came at length to hear of him, and taking ship to Quebec, sought out the young habitant and urged him to return with the vessel to New England. The young man, after long thought, decided to heed his kinsman and return to his own country. On a late summer's morning his goods were brought to the shores of the St. Lawrence where a small boat lay waiting to carry them to the ship, and presently the young man and his uncle took their places on the thwarts, and sailors began rowing from the shore. As the boat moved along the shore the young wife followed it on the beach, with one last appeal holding up their little son and crying out, "You may forsake me, but you cannot forsake your own flesh and blood." The young man could bear no more. Leaping into the river, he swam back to those whom he had thought of abandoning, and was not separated from his own.

The forest and the river, the forest with its paths and lakes, the river with its fierce currents and all the north beyond its shores—these are the theater of these eventful lives so full of courage and their own iron of integrity, so full of a sense of destiny and the strength of the human spirit.

CHAPTER FOUR

The Great Siege from the French Side of the Lines

I

THE eighteenth century on the Continent was an age of women. Women, not men, arranged its wars, putting on the casque of Bellona to music and sending out the armies with a word from a boudoir. Behind the official canvas of the formal history of the age, behind the vast abstractions called the nations, what reality sees are the Watteaulike figures of the queens and mistresses of the epoch, changing campaigns and ministries entirely at their pleasure and trumping each other's victories and successes with new victories and successes of their own. Drums beat, flags advanced into enemy fire, cannon thundered, and a note was sent for the hairdresser. In this terrible jeu de hasard of the palaces, this eager whist played without scruple in a famously unscrupulous age, the men without scruple joined with all pleasure and adroitness. Above the table the skill, genius, and alert blackguardism of Frederick the Great confronted with pleasure the intelligence and the opportunism of the Empress Maria Theresa of Austria, the Empress Elizabeth of Russia and the Marquise de Pompadour. At the end of the play, maps would be unrolled on a palace table, and a population change hands, and its children speak another language. The picture is neither romantic nor exaggerated. Great forces existed, it is true, but the direction of their power and even their very entrance into action could depend upon a whim, particularly at the court of Louis Quinze.

When Madame de Pompadour in her blue and rose ribbons became "maitresse en titre" in 1745 (that "morceau de roi" as her guardian once remarked) the War of the Austrian Succession had still three years to run. A confused affair of alien and foolish alliances which had involved Great Britain and almost the entire Continent, its crux was a struggle of Prussia against Austria for territorial gain. In this long duel, France, thanks to palace intrigue and to some meddling notion of "weakening" an Austria no longer dangerous, had entered as the ally of Frederick. The supremacy of France on the continent together with her colonial ambitions in North America had been hazarded for a Prussia cynically ready at any moment to take a cold-blooded advantage of any ally or power. At the close of hostilities, Frederick had kept his stolen Silesia and the French language had been enriched by a phrase which has never disappeared—"travailler pour Le Roi de Prusse"—*i.e.*, to make a fool of oneself for the advantage of another. The phrase was perhaps the only gain. So long a struggle, at once fierce and indecisive, had impoverished and shaken the entire state.

The fatal Seven Years' War, 1755-1763, began in a time of peace with a sudden attack on French shipping by the more powerful forces of Great Britain. Once again the European world dissolved, alliances and counter alliances coming into play, once again the white smoke of burning thatch rolled miserably up from the frontiers. Now occurred one of the most tragic mistakes of all European history. Changing partners at the palace gaming table—to continue the metaphor—France allied herself to the Austria of Maria Theresa, engaging herself to restore to Austria and the empress-queen the Silesian territory which the previous play had enabled Prussia to retain. Frederick, moving his chair with a sardonic gesture, had already allied himself with Britain. To balance this new alignment, the Empress of Russia now made it clear across the baize that she too had changed her mind, and in the new war would support both France and Austria. (Allied with Maria Theresa in the late contest, the Russians had marched a large and terrifying army to the Rhine frontiers of France—a foreshadowing of Napoleonic times.) Each a virtual autocrat, each all eagerness to win, the two empresses and Madame de Pompadour studied their hands and the interesting possibilities of play.

At the moment, France and Madame de Pompadour were one. Versailles was an absolutism, and the marquise controlled its powers. Established in the palace, magnificently housed with her secretaries, her lackeys and her cooks, she kept the king's bed, arranged dinners and nominated bishops, gave prestige to fashions, and directed both domestic and foreign policy. In his eternal boredom, his cureless listlessness and indifference, Louis the Fifteenth asked only that so charming and tireless a companion should continue to relieve him of the fatiguing task of being king. It is quite possible the madame thought she was saving the nation. Pretty, intelligent and unfailingly gay, the king-

dom was hers to do with as she would; she would see
what could be done. Was it not a little due to her taste
and discrimination that France in her time had become
for all Europe the arbiter of elegance, the glass of
fashion and the mold of form?

Committed to this tragic adventure on the Continent, to the designs of the tri-feminate, and faced
again with a second long war and a second press of ene-
mies, there was little France could do at sea. To rein-
force Canada and the faraway conquests in India would
be difficult indeed. In reality, there was but one enemy,
Great Britain. Ruled by an alert, intelligent and relentless oligarchy whose purposes were served heroically by
able and devoted men, the nation concerned itself with
its own proper advantage, seldom missing a trick. An
aristocratic command and ruthlessness pushed commerce ahead—it was the only life of the nation—and
as the trading vessels grew in number, so did the great
ships of the line. Confronting the three women in
power on the Continent, a fourth feminine figure,
metaphorical this time, gazed south across the straits
of Dover. It was Britannia as one saw her on the coins,
the seated figure with the shield, trident and lion, and
(could one but discern it) a sovereign eye on the sea and
the main chance.

In French Canada the bitterly cold winter of
1758 arrived on October 4th with a great fall of snow.
Three years of war had taxed all the resources of the
small population, but they had held their own. Food,
however, was now getting to be a problem. All the
previous summer so many colonists had been called
from their farms to the service of the king, that crops

had everywhere been scant: the coming winter would
be hungry. In the deserted roadstead of Quebec one last
French ship *La Sérieuse,* waited to carry overseas the
last dispatches of the year and a final appeal for aid.
De Bougainville (later to be the famous navigator) was
to present the petition at Versailles. The rims of the
St. Lawrence were already grim with ice when the ves-

sel sailed on November 12th, adventuring through the
fogs of Labrador and the British in the channel. Soon
afterwards the river closed. The grey quiescence of ice
hardened to iron, deepening beneath with every December night, storm after storm covering the level miles
with snow. Muffled in a military greatcoat and Canadian furs, an officer walked by himself on the Rue des
Remparts, sheltering himself from the icy wind blowing and eddying along the frozen plain. Some miles to
the east it was a plain no more, but a sea of packed
and broken floes carried to and fro past the winter-

covered mountains with the working of the tides. Burgesses of Quebec noted the figure and the favorite promenade. It was the king's commander in chief in Canada, the Marquis de Montcalm.

II

The sun was growing warm, and April and the heavy northern rains were clearing the land of snow and the river of its desert miles and deep solidities of ice. Lifted and broken from beneath by the spring floods, the floors of the stream had cracked, massing together in a doubled confusion of floes moving to sea along a channel daily widening. On the rock there had been a hard and hungry time. The official class and the small fashionable world, nevertheless, had continued their small provincial gaieties, innocent enough, and though this was felt to be a scandal by all, the French temperament was involved, and no one had been known to refuse an invitation. Now the ice was going out, and the days were at hand when the St. Lawrence turned for a while a benign and ocean blue. On May 10, 1759, a fleet of twenty-three vessels arrived safely before Quebec: it was de Bougainville returning, having again passed in the North Atlantic the cruising squadrons of the British fleet. From a France hard pressed on its own frontiers he had obtained the miserable little which could be shared, three hundred fresh recruits for the army, four engineers, twenty-three cannoneers, workmen, and armorers, and a smallish supply of arms and provisions. It was something—

New France had not been entirely abandoned—but it was not enough and the colony could do nothing but shrug its French and metaphorical shoulders and fight to the end. The situation at Versailles, to quote de Bougainville directly, could thus be put "The King, nothing: Madame everything."

As if a little ashamed of its shortcomings, the court had been prodigal of honors. The great men of the official world had all been given orders, ribbons, advances in grade, and royal approbation. Only Bigot, the scapegrace "intendant," had received a warning and a rap on the knuckles. More important than these parchments and jewels, however, were the dispatches and their news. A great British expedition, said the official script, was being prepared against Canada; indeed the main war effort of England would be directed against the colony. No matter what might happen, continued the voice of the ministry, it was of the utmost importance not to lose all. Somehow or other a foothold must be preserved in Canada.

The meeting of the challenge was to be the task of two capable professional soldiers of the eighteenth century wars, the Marquis de Montcalm and the Maréchal de Levis. By a happy chance these officers were not rivals but devoted personal friends. Montcalm had been in Canada since 1756. As a commander in chief he had been strikingly successful, having cleared the Ontario and Ticonderoga country of English footholds and invasions. Facing the tactical problem of campaigns in a wilderness, he had planned well and fought, as always, with the greatest personal bravery. (Years before he had been badly wounded in one of the great

European battles.) The skillful professional soldier, however, was but one side of the man; a private and personal life existed which he kept for his family and his friends, for his letters and the pages of a journal. These show us a man of forty-seven, father of ten children, a man of affectionate heart and loving phrase shadowed in spirit with the melancholy of four long years of separation. To his wife he wrote "To be eight months without a word . . . to love you more tenderly, my heart, would be impossible, and when will come my return? The day when I see you again will be the best of my life." And to Levis, "I try to kill time and amuse myself. . . . When will this drama we are acting in Canada come to its end? . . . Who the devil can say where we shall all be on November 1, 1759? . . . Without leaning on discouragement, I fear this campaign. . . . Went to a ball Tuesday last; don't take it that I found it very amusing." It is the French exile speaking, and the French bear exile with a pang. An officer recently arrived from France informed him one day that one of his daughters had died. Which daughter? The newcomer did not know. An able and experienced commander, a fine classical scholar, a philosophic exile, a devoted Catholic, such is the figure walking on the Rue des Remparts looking down on the channel in the ice. Presently the soldier would again take absolute command. "I venture to protest my entire devotion to save this unhappy colony or perish." The sentence is in a dispatch to Versailles and meant what it said.

No better a general than the marquis, Levis would appear to have been in temperament more the soldier.

Younger than Montcalm—only thirty-nine—he looks out at us from his portraits ready for anything, a preposterous court wig topping the congenial humanity of his soldier's head. The glance is direct and active, the features large and possessed of both character and breeding; it is the countenance of a nobleman and soldier who could manage the etiquette of a court as well as the difficulties of a redoubt in Flanders. Such men like action not only for its own sake but also because it provides for them a means of expression. Levis was not a victim of the pensiveness which troubled Montcalm. On the contrary, the sense of danger put him on his mettle and gave him heart. Indeed, it was in these same tense days of the late spring that he wrote to a kinswoman in France suggesting that she look about for him in the world and find him a wife.

The British armada had sailed, and the coming problem of the French command was the defense of a naturally strong position with insufficient forces and supplies. French coureurs de bois and their wild, tobacco-brown Indian allies, newly arrived infantrymen from mother France with mosquito-bitten faces, fishermen and eelcatchers from the river, habitant levies and recruits in their peasant homespun, sailors from merchant ships and the navy, burgesses from Quebec and the shops of the lower town—all these were to be swiftly made into an army and set to work. (Nothing could be done till the earth was open.) Under the watchful glance of Montcalm, a system of defense presently began to take form. The danger would come from the river, and to prevent a landing and an attack, a continuous fortified line, a camp retranché of the eighteenth century military texts, began at a redoubt on the St. Charles and continued east eight miles to the Falls of the Montmorency, occupying the crest of the great escarpment falling hundreds of feet to the river-level flats and meadows of the tidal St. Lawrence. Small forts and outposts were also built closer about the city. Few military positions can have been as naturally superb as these great lines at Beauport. Tossing their shovels of earth, the soldiers, the citizens, and the coureurs de bois must have wondered what Wolfe and Messieurs les Anglais would do when faced with such a line.

A growing tension gathered in the city. Special masses were said in all the churches, and under the pale sunlight of May, religious processions made the tour of the walls, filling the provincial streets with the dignity of ecclesiastical pomp and the choral singing of the psalms.

On May 22nd, Montcalm returned in the early evening from a journey to Montreal, and went directly to his house on the Rue des Remparts. Delayed against his will at Montreal, he had had to spend the last day of his journey home making a forced march along the hard going of the river roads.

To give warning of the approach of the enemy, a line of beacons had been prepared along the great capes of the Laurentians, the dry fagots and the coils of birchbark waiting under lean-tos for the sudden flint and steel. Wilderness league upon league, headland by headland above the vast rain-colored stream, above the white islands of the fog by day and the cold sunsets of the north, men in homespun watched the direction of the gulf for some first sail in the mist, for some first light appearing on the sea.

Montcalm had busied himself all the 23rd with important conferences. Meeting at the intendant's palace with the officers of the port and the officers of the king's ships, he had approved a decision to build a floating battery, and send three hundred sailors ashore to work on the defensive lines by the St. Charles. At midnight an officer of the guard, conducted by Montcalm's servant, knocked at his bedroom door. It was a clear night, and all along the St. Lawrence the beacon fires were burning on the heights. From Baie St. Paul to Cap Tourmente, they spaced the wall of the night and the overhanging darkness, by small bright point and nearer blaze burning fiercely on the great sides of the mountains. The expedition against Canada had arrived in the St. Lawrence, and as a first group of ships came to a first anchorage under the Laurentians, the rattle of chain forged in the navy yards of England presently woke the early morning quiet of the Île aux Coudres.

III

It was a formidable armada. With its ships of war, its transports, and its vessels of supply, with its regiments and cannon and naval and military stores, the expedition was the greatest which had ever left behind the shores of England. Some hundred and fifty ships housing an assembled force of twelve thousand men were making their way into the narrowing reaches of the river. A microcosm of England and Scotland had been waiting to see Canada 'appear. Staff officers military and naval walking the decks in fine weather, Scot regiments talking their own rustic tongue then so much more prodigious to an English ear, a civilian artist, a guest of Wolfe's, in eighteenth century snuff-brown, surgeons, armorers, gunners, engineers and seamen—this was the world under the great canvases swaying against the sky. The armada had sailed from Britain by fleets and smaller squadrons, some leaving early, others following after, and crossing the Atlantic with uneven speed and fortune, had managed a rendezvous at Louisburg. (A first flotilla had found the Cape Breton region clogged with ice and had had to enter Halifax.) Not a vessel had been lost. It was from Louisburg that the reassembled ships had sailed out to turn the Gaspé, and the Canadian and Breton fishermen of the peninsula had seen them pass from the towers of the cliffs.

Only the cold tenacity of Pitt, only that austere and almost disembodied will playing its relentless game of chess with continents and nations, could ever have assembled so great a force. By the close of summer, however, it was essentially a defeated power. Months had passed, part of May, June, July and August, the expedition had attempted what was seemingly possible and was still busy trying out indecisive maneuvers, the villages on the river lay for miles in blackened and tragic ruin, and yet Quebec stood untaken on its rock. Already the autumnlike premonition of cold seldom absent from mid-August on the river had come into the huge air, and those on the ships who held the middle watch must have seen the shoulders of Orion slanting above the wilderness and rising in the sky. So little time remained. The famously difficult navigation of the river and the gulf would presently enter upon its most hazardous season, and so great an expedition could not run an improper risk of general shipwreck and disaster.

In a house at Ange Gardien, in an habitant farm which may be seen today, Wolfe, the very soul and vital spirit of the force, lay deathly sick and helpless of a fever. He had never been physically strong. From his sickbed he could hear the distant cannon on the heights of Point Levis firing across the river into the heart of Quebec. (A British landing had carried the heights of Levis on July 19th.) The small compact city was melting away under the rain of steel and fire. On every street shattered houses, unroofed and burnt, stood in hollow ruin, the tragic shell of the Cathedral still standing gaunt and broken above the general wreck. Those who could do so had moved their household goods to a place of safety in the country; there had been days in the warmth of July when a confusion of carts and wagons laden with furniture had almost clogged the narrow streets. The summer had been really hot, and fierce thunderstorms had broken over the rock, mingling the artillery of heaven with the flames and smoke of the English fire bombs. The city was dying—but the fortress was another matter: it remained alive and in power, and the expedition was no nearer its capture than it had been in May.

Most troubling thought of all, a thought which gave no peace to the sick man in his bed, a great battle had been fought and lost. Studying and studying again his maps and plans of the magnificent natural situation, Wolfe had decided that willy-nilly a frontal attack must be made on the French positions. The signal for the assault had been given on the morning of July 31st. It had been a fine morning with a handy southwest breeze which had helped the ships work inshore and favored a landing from the boats. The troops had advanced with fine courage to the difficult attack of the slopes and heights, and a careful plan of feints and ruses had gone into action to confuse and divide the enemy. The British cannon had thundered from the ships, the shore batteries and entrenchments had replied, and all up and down the steep hillsides and the almost plunging descents, the rural scene of the northern parishes had crackled and crashed with desperate and continuous gunfire. On the British side the troops had held with tenacity to their almost impossible task; on the French side, the king's regiments and the habitant detachments had fought with the old French wildness, the "furia Francese" of the bygone chronicles. Levis, the fighting soldier, had been at his best; now mounted, now afoot, he had been everywhere, the whitish cannon smoke blowing past him up the slopes from the batteries below. All day long the British had come on, daring the dreadful climb. All day long the sound of battle had rolled inland towards the timeless emptiness of the northern wilderness. Then, at five o'clock, nature had helped history decide. A sudden thunderstorm had broken over the valley, loosing its sheets of drenching Laurentian rain, and hiding man from man in the folds of the torrents and the dark. The hillsides had turned to slopes of water and trampled grass, to slippery and precipitous paths of mud, tragic with the

motionless dead and the fury of the rain. Wolfe had
sounded the retreat. The battle of Montmorency had
been fought and lost. Some better scheme, some sounder
plan of battle would have to be found.

In the rainy night, the French wounded streamed
back to the hospitals of the city. Through the ruined
streets came the fierce and painted Indians with their
wounds bound in rags, young officers from Paris, riding or hobbling, and the patient habitant farmer with
a son to give him aid. Rows of pallets had been prepared for them in the safety of the deeper cellars of
the rock, and all night long the Ursulines and the
women of religion had tended them, walking with their
candles the long gloom of the vaults and going with
their bandages and medicines from figure to figure laid
along the floor.

Presently the ebbing summer turned the corner of
August and September. From the heights of Quebec
Montcalm studied and watched every move and maneu-
ver of the expedition still holding to the river. A fine
classical scholar, he described what he saw in a phrase
which has a classical quality. "In the distance of the
Isle of Orleans," he wrote, "I saw the forest of great
ships."

At the end of August a sudden message had come
from the west, of approaching danger on "the frontier". Enemy forces from the American colonies were
moving north. Meeting in the early night at the Manoir
Salaberry, the French "quartier general", a council of
officers had decided that de Levis must go at once and
take command. By nine o'clock the marshal and a companion were already on their way through the sharp

cold of the night. Deprived of his best soldier, of his trusted counselor and friend, Montcalm knew that he must now hold Quebec alone.

IV

It was September, and Wolfe had risen from his bed, a wan figure gloomily occupied in staring at the river and wondering what next to do. Writing from the cabin of a British man-of-war on a day of cold autumnal squalls and rain, he set down these discouraged words in a report to England: "I am sufficiently restored to be able to do my duty, but my health is entirely ruined without the consolation of having rendered any considerable service to the state and without the perspective of being able to render any." So cold and forlorn was the weather that anxiety was felt for the health of the troops. Sharing the same wind and rain, the French shivered in their miles of entrenchments, whilst on the rock itself the storm swept along the empty streets drenching the burnt and deserted ruins. The arrival of autumn and the consequent possibility that the siege might be raised had a little cheered the city, but the French staff was under no illusions. Whatever the weather and the calendar might be doing, the danger was still present and very great, and the tension poignant and continuous.

For some time the British had been succeeding in passing the narrows of the rock and taking the ships into the reaches west of the town. Rainy nights and the St. Lawrence darkness and fog had favored these adventures but now they were being made with every

helpful turn of the wind and with an almost scornful daring. On September 4th a whole convoy of boats, baggages and munitions passed the narrows. One of those decisions so frequently encountered in military history, those curious decisions which seem to be made by an army itself rather than by any commander or council of war, was coming into being. Wolfe had thought of various schemes, notions rather than plans which he had talked over with his brigadiers but nothing had crystallized or turned itself into energy and action. The sense of defeat had not lifted from his heart. Now the whole imagination and effort of the expedition was turning in power to the west of the city, Wolfe himself leading and sharing the new hopes. Fleets of barges now lay west of the narrows, and day after day the troops based on Levis extended their power westward along the south shore of the river. In a ship's boat rowed by a crew from a man-of-war, Wolfe himself studied the western reach, scanning with his glass the untaken rock and the tumbling slopes and precipices fronting on the river. On one such expedition, it is said, he observed women washing clothes at a beach below the cliffs, and noted with interest that the linen was being spread to dry on the bushes above. This he took to mean that not too difficult a path must there ascend the rock.

The 9th was vaporous and warm, a touch of August returning with the southwest wind; uncertain weather followed and another clearing. It was decided that the night of the 12th should see the attack. The swift and tragic climax was at hand. A curious continuity, a kind of fatality of events brought the action to its resolution. On the 12th two French deserters from the regiment known as the Royal Roussillon, being questioned at British headquarters, admitted that the path Wolfe had suspected actually did exist, and that the cove he had seen (l'Anse du Foulon) was but poorly guarded. Moreover, and somewhat à propos des bottes, they informed their captors that on that very night a train of French barges was to descend the river with supplies for the troops at Beauport. Wolfe saw and seized his chance. He would precede this convoy with his convoy of troops and station some French-speaking officer ahead to hoax the sentinels. The French boatmen of the convoys were in the habit of holding close to the northern shore, clinging for secrecy and protection to the double darkness of the narrows and the over-hanging gloom of the great cliffs. Now chance enters again. Unknown to Wolfe, the French train of barges due to pass on the night of the 12th, had been sud-denly countermanded. By some appalling mischance, however, or carelessness beyond all reproof, news of the change in orders had not been passed on to the sentinels in the coves. They expected a train of barges, and one they had. But the boats were Wolfe's.

Afloat on the vast blackness of the river, in silence and the night following the vague presence of the French shore, the barges glide downstream. It is one o'clock in the morning. The sky is moonless, the stars are veiled with mist. Seated in a smaller boat, one of a small group of figures scarce visible to each other in the dark, Wolfe recites to his companions the noble and melancholy quatrains of Gray's "Elegy." It is to this solemn music, to these cadenced and antique lines that the curtain rises on one of the greatest decisions in all human history. The issue is not alone power over a con-tinent or the end of a rivalry of race and tongue; more than events are at stake. Something of the very nature of the century to come is here engaged, even something of the quality of its values of life together with the horizons of its imagination. Meanwhile between the dark of the river and the other dark of earth, the voice closes in solemnity.

> " 'The boast of heraldry, the pomp of power,
> And all that beauty, all that wealth e'er gave,
> Await alike the inevitable hour:
> The paths of glory lead but to the grave.'

"Gentlemen, I would rather have written those lines than take Quebec."

A voice speaking out of the dark made a first challenge of the boats as they passed the part of the shore called Samos.

"Qui vive?"

"France," answered the captain of Fraser's Highlanders, he who spoke so good a French. And he added, make no noise, these are the provisions; we might be heard. "Ne faites pas de bruit, ce sont les vivres."

"Passez!"

There was no request for the password, no coming down to the shore to make sure of the identity of the speaker.

A moment later, a little farther along the cliffs, and the troops are landing. So unguarded were the heights that not a single gunshot disturbed the enclosing silences as the little army scrambled up the easy path. The dawn began to pale. At first there were clouds and a few light showers. Far above the river and the gorge, Wolfe's regiments re-formed, gathering quietly into companies. So easy and unharassed was the hour, that save for the wild American scene of rock and bush, the red-coated infantry and the Highlanders

in their plaids might well have thought themselves at
morning drill in England.

V

Montcalm had passed an uneasy night. To confuse
the French and cover the attack preparing to the west,
the British had made the 12th a long day of feints,
maneuvers and inexplicable comings and goings. The
whole fleet had been in movement on the river. One
great squadron sailing to and fro from position to position had presented a continuous threat of action, forc-
ing the French to move detachments about with little
chance of rest, and keep pace with them along the river.
At French headquarters this general activity of the
enemy had been held to foreshadow a possible second
attack on the fortified outer lines, and all night long
there had been apprehension at Beauport. Now the
morning was at hand, and all seemed peaceful again.
The same forest of ships lay at anchor in the great
roadstead, waking in its own time to the grey sky and
the same small showers of early morning rain. Having
risen about sunrise, Montcalm swung himself on a
favorite horse and rode off to have an early riser's cup
of tea with his friend the Chevalier Johnstone, then
billeted at the Seminary of La Canardière by the western lines. The unceasing bombardment of Quebec had
taken on a particular fury. The thunder of cannon
from Levis rolled heavily in the air. It was while he
was drinking this awakening cup that the first news
reached him of the landing of the British. Hurrying
down the seminary corridors to the breakfast table, an

officer from the French post nearest the Anse du Foulon arrived with his appalling tidings. The British were on the heights.

The first thing to be done was to make sure of what had happened and to gather and rally all the forces of the defense. The morning became a time of dispatches, hasty orders and short conferences, a time of bugle calls and the beat of the French drum. Such news as arrived was bad. Wolfe had marched towards the city and chosen his field of battle, the cleared land of the Plains of Abraham, and there behind entrenchments was waiting for the French. An advance party of coureurs de bois and Canadian sharpshooters had crept towards them from the city and were harassing them, Indian style, from ambush. Montcalm's first glance at the situation was one of dismay. He had hoped and perhaps expected to find himself confronted by a part of Wolfe's army, but here was the whole of it, scarlet rank on rank, together with such cannon as it could shoulder and tug up the sides of the rock.

It was ten o'clock: the day had cleared and the sun was shining. His army of French regulars, Canadian levies, and coureurs de bois formally in line, Montcalm gave the order to sound the charge. Crisp and military, the notes rang out in the tense air, the cannon firing from Levis thundering their distant undertone. Rock and hill, the gorge of the vast river, and the blue morning sky next shook with a first crashing as the French advanced and the scarlet lines advanced to meet them. Timing their fire well, and massing it with terrible effect, standing up magnificently to the more impetuous French fusillade, the British held the shock; a first

current, a first small ripple of the tide of victory turning their way at the beginning. Smoke drifted over the
plain, sulphurous and pungent, flowing aerial over the
dead still warm, the outcries of battle, the terror, the
exultation, and the shock. The simultaneous volleys
crashed and the wild single shots; the artillery roaring
out its screaming missiles through the human and unhuman storm of sound. Suddenly the French broke.
Regulars and levies, coureurs de bois, and Indians in
their battle fantasies of paint could stand no more, and
in a moment growing swifter as it came to its resolution, there was no longer an army. Towards the city
it fled, a crowd of fugitives in fast and furious dis-
order. Shouts of triumph, wild English halloos and
fierce Scottish cries of war rose from the British lines,
and the victorious army went forward in a rush.

Montcalm, caught in the melee and borne alone
by its stream, had been forced back to the Porte St.
Louis. The beginning of the battle had seen him riding
before his battle line, his right arm extended and his
sword leveled towards the enemy, calling to the French
in his men with the formal gesture of the rhetoric
of war. At the gate, bullets were coming fast, spatter-
ing on the stones in fusillades of English lead. Struggling in the crowd and maneuvering as he could his
uneasy horse, the commander sought to turn the fugitives. Suddenly two bullets struck him almost simul-
taneously, one in the armpit, another in the thigh. The
blood began to flow down his saddle and over his horse's
side. Three soldiers now caught him up and held him
on his horse, and fought their way with him into the
Rue St. Louis. Some women cried out in pity as he

passed, but the dying man soothed them with an assurance and a courtesy. "It is nothing, it is nothing; do not
trouble yourselves for me, good friends."

At the house of the Surgeon Arnoux on the Rue
St. Louis, they made him as comfortable as they could.
It chanced that Arnoux himself was absent from the
city, serving somewhere with the army, so "the young
Arnoux" his brother, also a surgeon, had care of the
wounded man. During the afternoon Montcalm remained strong enough to keep in touch with the situation and even dictate various short letters and dispatches. Then came a time when he could or would
do no more. "No," said he, "I have no orders or ad-
vices to give, the time left to me is very short, and
now I must turn myself to even more important
things."

The night of battle closed about the city all darkness and cold. Quebec was still New France; there had
been no surrender. In the same cold and quiet, in a
tent to one side of his troops and the small cautious
fires, Wolfe lay dead, mourned by every man of his
command. A certain shy thoughtfulness, a certain courtesy of the grand manner had touched their hearts and
imaginations, and he had led them himself into battle
walking ahead of them towards the volleys of the
enemy. On the other side of the wall, through the ruin
in the narrow streets, the aged saint and courtly gentle-
man who was then bishop of Quebec, Msgr. de Pont-
briand, came to give the sacraments to Montcalm, and
receive his last messages for the family so far away in
France. The town was still, heavy with a stricken quiet,
but now and again the confusion at its heart betrayed

itself with some noise heard sudden in the night, a voice, the hurry of steps, a moment's sound of the wheels of a cart.

At dawn, Montcalm had gone his way, his head sunken in the great French pillow, his swollen shoulder troubling him no more. Looking again at his portrait, at that composed, intelligent face which has something

of the paterfamilias above the eighteenth century armor, one would wish that he might have met with a kindlier fate in the wilderness of the New World, returning to France and his own hearth not without honor, there to hang his sword on the wall, and read his Latin poets by an evening fire.

Three more days remained of the French flag. The situation was past saving; the army was broken, some of it had already gone home, and there was no food for soldier or civilian. Flanking the rock on its landward side, the British had reached the lines of the St. Charles, imprisoning the desolated city on its wilderness acropolis. In the autumnal cold, refugees from below were huddling in every shelter or standing forlorn in the open streets about their fires; the hospitals were crowded with the wounded and dying. There is a peace of defeat as well as a peace of victory, and the mood of the city could not be stirred from the dignity of its passive despair. "Nous étions sauvés et nous sommes perdus," as the French officer wrote so poignantly in a memoir of the time. For two days torrential rains fell, gathering all into darkness between the sea wrack above and the drenched wilderness below; then, with a change of wind, came blue skies and the sun. Just before sundown on the 18th, the gates of the city opened, and General Townsend and his staff walked through the lengthening shadows to the open square before the Château St. Louis. The last troops of France in power at Quebec stood drawn up in line before the building, her last sentries were posted at its door. A pause, a roll of drums and the French commander of the castle tendered the keys of the city to the victors. Cannon sounded, and the flag of Great Britain broke out on the west wind. The little tableau of eighteenth century ceremony was the last of old France upon the rock.

Later in the dusk, those of Quebec who lived by the Place St. Louis saw young British officers returning to look in evening quiet at the great view of the river to the east. The far mountains and the horizons beyond the ships, the burnt villages where no light would show, the Isle of Orleans dark on the dividing streams of the incomparable river, the vast forest to the south uniting with the colonies, all this was now theirs to rule. The St. Lawrence was no longer a highway of Versailles: the distant rays of that faraway world of fashion, wit, and civilized intelligence would no longer strike along those wildnerness eddies and the vast outpouring of the lakes. The French colonist and his hearth, the coureur de bois in the forest, the Indian and his lodge—battle had won them for London to be a part of Bow Bells and the Exchanges, new riches of the Johnsonian world of great merchants and houses on the Thames, clubs and the best of talk, the Whig aristocracy and the British fleet at anchor in the Downs. (The same Versailles would presently give over the keys of India.) East of the rock and west, a thousand miles of the river and the sea, things almost timeless and things united with history and time waited together for the morning to come.

CHAPTER FIVE

The Golden Age of the Canoe

I

THE revival of the fur trade began at Montreal. Following the great capitulation, the old French town had died back into itself, its French capital fled, its French organization broken, its ruling world of French colonial officials gone forever overseas. Even the fur trade had dimmed into a memory. In the region of its commerce and the wharves shutters covered the doors and windows of the old French merchants: the waiting ships, the Norman drays and the great, corded, animal-smelling bales were a part of life no more. The little which remained alive of France in the west was to be found at the French stations on the Lakes. Here a French population of canoemen and trappers stood by their settlements, keeping the French flag boldly flying and wondering where next to turn. Winters came and went, the great fresh-water seas froze their pale and leaden white under their leaden overpall, and the outpost world remained by its canoes and waited for a sign.

Presently a call for action was sounded from beyond Niagara by new masters and a new race. An almost national invasion of Scots—McTavishes, Mackenzies, McDonells and McLeods, names to make Quintilian stare and gasp—had arrived in Montreal and begun the economic revival of the city. The principal

76

business of the port, the western fur trade, had naturally their first attention, and an enterprising and somewhat confused reorganization woke the commerce to new life. For a time companies rose, companies fell, and companies melted together in a kaleidoscope of titles and directors. By the 1780's and the 1790's, however, the trade had come into its second wind. The French at the Lakes who had joined the system early now had charge of the exploring and carrying: the Scots at Montreal planning the campaigns, maintaining the organization, and keeping the books. With the pooling of Montreal interests in 1787 and the formation of a first Northwest Company arrived a nabob's era of prosperity.

(Delivered of French rivalry by the capitulation, and scarce aware of the new competition, the "sleeping giant" of the north, the great company of Hudson's Bay, dozed in its arctic greyness of fog, but it had life in its somnolence and was later to awaken in energy and power.)

Once more the shutters were down. The warehouses open, ships at the wharves, and furs arriving from the wilderness. So began one of the great episodes of Canada and North America—the Golden Age of the Canoe.

II

The "canoe" we know today, though in a general sense the gift of the Algonquin tribes of the northeast, is more particularly a Chippewa creation, a Chippewa masterpiece. Living in the heart of the old canoe-birch country, every man of the nation with his eye and mark on some great tree, the tribe united as no other a special skill in design with the finest of materials. The lovely curve of bow and stern remains for us their sign. Every Indian nation of the birch region had its own native and tenacious image of that bold symmetry. Some made of it a quasi perpendicular, some put the depth here, others there: a stranger could be placed by the line of his canoe as easily as by the cut of his moccasins. To the Chippewas alone was reserved the sense of the curve in its perfection, in its unique and beautiful rightness. Strong, well-made, capable of carrying heavy loads yet easy to portage, the Chippewa model like the covered wagon is a part of the history of the continent.

This was the craft which was to make possible the opening and mapping of something like a fourth of North America. In celebrating the covered wagon we have forgotten a little this episode of the canoe. Enlarged by its Indian builders for the fur trade of the old Canadian northwest, it kept its Chippewa character and strength, making itself a vessel for cargoes and crews without losing one touch of its old beauty of design.

Three principal types were in use in the trade. The great Montreal canoe or "canot du maitre", intended for use on the larger lakes and more navigable streams could be anywhere between thirty and forty-five feet long. Such a vessel could carry tons of furs eastward from the posts. Fourteen men made up the crew. The north canoe, or "canot du nord," was a smaller type; built for use in the wilderness itself, it averaged twenty-five feet in length and carried a crew of eight. Between these familiar models stood an intermediate third, the bastard, or "le batard", which carried a crew of ten. Small canoes such as we know today were also everywhere in use. To judge by many old pictures and sketches, sails were sometimes rigged, being most probably raised up on occasions when it was possible to "sail before the wind" in light airs.

The canoe workshops remained in the birch country and on the Lakes. Once built, the canoes of the trade went in for that liveliness of color which is so good for the soul. It was not for nothing that the later eighteenth century had rediscovered and enlarged the bright possibilities of paint. Gunwales were festooned or spaced in green and white or in red and white, and there was almost invariably a design of some kind—an Indian head, a bear, a sun or a moon with features, clasped hands—painted bow and stern. The paddles of strong red cedar were also painted with stripes and gaieties.

A carry down the beach into the placid water of some cove and the craft was ready for its man. He was at hand. Hardy and enduring as few strains have been in history, unwashed, merry, and famously polite, short of legs and powerful of shoulder, pure French now, and now half Indian, the canoe had already invented its own human being, the woods their man, the legendary and incomparable voyageur.

III

Westward beyond the great horizons of Superior, westward beyond the strange, jade-green waters and the tense yet empty wind, westward a thousand and even a long two thousand miles away, the forts and stations of the fur companies stood in the immense solitudes of the forest. From the dying out of the great plains north to the arctic barrens, from the Lakes west to the mountain descents to the Pacific, the wilderness spread wide over a solitude of the continent, a region of lakes and woods, rapids and rushing rivers, bogs and quaking swamps and mountains without a name. Within, there lay hidden a complexity, some valleys and forest floors teeming with life, others strangely with scarce a sign of any thing alive. Till the arrival of the fur trade, nothing which was not a part of nature disturbed a quiet of nature widespread and empty as the sky. Only the nomad Indians of the American north, the Dene, the hardy Chippewa, the Crees, and the western Montagnais were a part of its existence, crossing it with scarce the bending of a branch or a footprint in the leaves.

A great skein of waterways leading west and north out of Lake Superior was the gateway to the mystery. Indians had been the first to use the passage, tying river to lake and lake to river again, and the French had been aware of it since 1731, La Verendrye and his guides having gone in as far as the Lac des Bois.

By the end of the eighteenth century, the fur trade had chosen and made customary a great passage to the woods known as the "Great Trace." It began at Montreal with the waters above Lachine, and entering the Ottawa ascended that stream of many portages to the Mattawa, a tributary flowing from the west. This in turn led to Lake Nipissing, and from Nipissing, hailing with a cheer a westward-flowing stream, the voyageurs descended to Georgian Bay and the waters of the Lakes. The charming island of Michilimackinac, depot and administrative station of the trade upon the Lakes, next awaited the adventurers: here the "brigades" going into the deeper wilderness separated from those bound to nearer posts. So distant were many stations that it took the best of summer to arrive, and the voyageurs wintered at the forts.

All summer long the pretty island was a scene of bustle and activity. Goods were transshipped, crews sorted out and reassembled, the sick attended to, and canoes repaired. Standing on the heights at night, looking out into the vast darkness above Huron, one could see fires burning all up and down the lower beach, each glow of fire crowded close about with its own company.

For those bound north and west, the next great station was Grand Portage on the western shore of Superior. (It is today a town in Minnesota just below the Canadian frontier.) Here nine miles of rapids on the St. Francis River made necessary a long carry. In the great days of the trade homemade roads had been built at the carry, and a score of wagons and several hundred horses assisted the voyageur crews to move their goods and canoes to the navigable waters. Ahead lay the entering chain of lake and river widenings, the Lac du Bois Blanc, the Lac de la Pluie, the Lac des Bois and, ultimately, the great lake "Ouinnipique." Beyond lay the unknown, the white streams and the forest-brown, the named and the unnamed, the peaceful and the perilous. At dangerous rapids there were always crosses to be seen against the forest wall, each with its voyageur's cap fading in the sun.

Standing near the greater portages and by the junctions of streams, the forts of the trade awaited their first arriving hail.

Each had its chief, or "bourgeois," usually a Scot, each its tallymen, clerks, and accountants, each its population forever changing and mingling, of trappers and hunters, half-breed children and Indian wives, voyageurs, scouts, and forest adventurers. The Indians and half-breeds were usually the trappers, taking the animals in winter when the pelts were at their best. In the spring, bands would arrive with their catch, the furs hanging behind them from their shoulders. Such a population lived as it could. Now buffalo meat and deer went into the pot, now flour, grease, wild rice, and a bear's haunch all cooked together into some hearty Indian mess. (An Indian stew can last for years, seemingly recreating itself miraculously from the bottom of the pot.) With nothing but the forest about it for a thousand miles the fort lived its vigorous life of direct contacts, slept in its blankets and buckskins, drank its rum, smoked its tobacco, wrestled out its male rivalries, listened to its interminable Indian legends, and married "according to the custom of the country". Parentage could be vague. "Que voulez-vous? What d'ye want, laddie?" said one Scot trader to an Indian boy. "Monsieur," replied the youngster with gravity, "vous êtes mon père."

French was the common tongue. Wild and outlandish as such a life must have been it is clear that it did not become barbarous. The natural good manners and sociability of the French Canadian kept it all a remarkably good-tempered adventure. It was with a gesture of politeness that one was offered a little more of the bear.

With portages to make and currents to battle, with loads of supplies to carry in and heavy furs to carry out, with the wilderness for a country and elemental danger ever near, the life of a voyageur was no adventure for the weak. In good weather and when not fighting a wind or a stream a crew could paddle fantastic distances. Between earliest dawn and summer's dark, canoes often managed sixty, seventy or even eighty miles. One observer speaks of about forty strokes of the paddle to the minute,—a brisk rhythm and speed. Two meals a day were eaten and after a hard carry, a third. They ate everything. Pemmican, fish, birds' eggs and almost any kind of bird, hawks among them, squirrels, porcupines, dough cakes and grease dumplings —all these were downed with relish by the evening fire.

The contemporaries of the voyageurs who accompanied them on their expeditions above all remembered the singing of the crews. Mile after mile they sang, singing together with the thrust of their swift strokes, the gay, choral sound echoing back upon them from the enclosing walls of the forest or floating off across the stillness of lakes into the north and the unknown. It was ever a cheerful sound, a sound of labor and the human spirit, a music of the body's good will and the heart's content. Old ballads and songs of France made up the substance of the singing, most of them unchanged in verse or tune, though now and then a wind from the spruces had blown across a song making it more Canadian in its language and mood. It is a man's world which is here reflected; its concerns are going

courting, the formal elegancies of wooing, the pains
of youth and broken hearts, and noble and ceremonious
farewells. Nothing can exceed their decorum. To this
pleasant and old-fashioned treasury the voyageur came
in time to add new songs of his own but the old songs
remained his favorites. If they were not Canadian in the
beginning, he made them Canadian by adding himself.

So the cavaliers bow, sweeping off their seventeenth century hats to tunes made for harpsichords,
the lover laments, and the soldier returns from the wars.
And all the while the forest passes by, the white water
rolls over the rock, the sides of the canoe scrape with a
rasp through the pitcher plants, and the paddles dip
and thrust and rise gleaming together in the sun.

IV

No adventure of the Canadian past so stirred the
heart as the departure of the voyageurs from their
depot at Lachine. One came upon them in the busy
spring, some camping by the river in the open fields,
Montreal and its church bells behind them to the east,
and before them the afternoon sun and the adventure
of the west. For days before the embarkation wagons
had been arriving with their loads, rolling through the
farming villages and deepening the ruts and puddles
with their weight of trade goods, provisions and supplies. In and out of the offices and wharves, busy at a
hundred tasks, yet always finding a moment to toss
back a jest, swarmed the adventurers, a whole French-
Canadian countryside of Gaspards, Aurèles, Onesimes,
and Hippolytes. There was much to be done. Here, on

the beach, men crouched by a canoe making some last repair, here clerks scrambled over boxes and bags checking and rechecking the trading goods, the trinkets, beads, axes, knives, awls, blankets, and bolts of bright red English flannel, here an official studied the enlistment papers of some new engagé. At a counter to one side, a crowd selected the shirts, trousers, handkerchiefs, and blankets due them from the company, Iroquois Indians from Caughnawaga, famous paddlemen, reaching in and seizing with the rest. Late in the afternoon, those who were quiet over a pipe could hear the eternal murmur of the miles of rapids, and the floating, clanging summons of the Angelus.

The moment of departure waited upon weather and the wind. To prevent a last and too-thirsty festival of farewell, efforts were sometimes made to conceal the probable day, but men concerned have sixth sense in these matters, and the world was apt to share the secret, and all Montreal, finding the morning fair, came to say good-bye. Ladies with escorts watched from the shores, British officers, mounted on English horooflooh rode to good places in the fields, British soldiers even, their flaxen hair and blue Sussex eyes a new note in the throng, strolled in pairs among the Indians. Citizens and citizenesses, wives and children, parents and kin, company directors and curés—all these were at hand to see the start. It was early May, and the Montreal country had left winter behind and was taking courage in the spring; on far shores and near, under the cool wind, appeared the green.

In and out of the press, heroes of the occasion, moved the voyageurs. Old hands and new, it was their day. Even the young Scot clerks who were to go as passengers to the forts shared the importance and the glory. Custom demanding that the beginning and end of a journey should be carried off in style, every voyageur was dressed in the best he had. A woolen tunic or long shirt worn outside and belted about with a bright, home woven sash—the charming, old-fashioned ceinture flèchee—Indian leggings or even homespun trousers, a red knitted cap, and heavy-duty Indian moccasins—this was the costume. A beaded Indian pouch worn at the waist, Iroquois or Chippewa work, was a particular *sine qua non:* indeed, all veterans were engayed with Indian finery. Voyageurs belonging to the governor or chief factor's brigade had feathers in their caps. Often a small British flag was flown from each canoe. The fleet sailed by "brigades", by groups under one command, and these kept together, maneuvering with careful paddles in the current falling to the Lachine. Are all afloat, all loaded, all officers and passengers in their seats? Then go! Church bells rang, guns were fired, and on the broad river paddles dipped and thrust forward in a first strong, beautiful and rhythmic swing. At the same moment the river covered itself with singing. The fleet beginning to open, the brigades sorting out, one could see nothing but canoes for miles, hundreds upon hundreds of the laden craft all striking as one into the purplish-brown waters of the Ottawa.

At the northwestern corner of Montreal Island stood a church of Ste. Anne, patroness of sailors and of voyageurs. Here the brigades made a first halt and landing, the paddlemen and bowsmen, the steersmen, clerks and passengers all trooping up from the beach to pray for a safe voyage and a safe return. It was the custom to make some small offering, and the Scot Presbyterians it is said, made theirs in propriety with the rest. Soon they were all of them on the river again, the church hidden by some turn of the stream, some brigades falling into their measure and stroke, some out of high spirits leaping ahead with a song. "En roulant, ma boule, roulant," and out of sight they go. Thrust by thrust, by quiet waters and by furious streams, through the summer plague of the stinging flies and the blessed coming of the early cold, the paddles will swing across the half of a continent, making their way into the forest, into the land of Keewaytin, the northwest wind, the ancient land where nothing has changed since the beginning of the world.

CHAPTER SIX

Old French Canada

I

THE long years with their long winters had come and gone, and the summers with the wheat ripening to gold between the river and the spruce. In the garrison towns a Gallic and ancestral din of bells had long mingled with a familiar, even a reassuring, beat of British drums. Outwardly, the ancien régime had vanished from the land even as the smoke from the burning farms and houses of Quebec had at length faded from sight above the cooling walls, and beyond the Labrador fog and the intervening sea, it had likewise died in France. The bloodiest of revolutions had there taken it by the throat, burning its thrones and altars, and tossing its plumes and pretty femininities to the derision of the street. The tombs of the kings, even the peace of the dead, had been violated. In one dreadful week the royal monuments of Saint-Denis had been opened one after the other, and kings, queens, princes and princesses tumbled out one after the other into a ditch. Louis XIV, still in his periwig, was, so they all noted, perfectly preserved, but in visage "black as ink". What had the people of the St. Lawrence to do with this glare from overseas, these far-off outcries and hootings, the ready torrents of rhetoric and the curiously cold-blooded intellectually dramatized massacres? What

patriotic exultation could they be supposed to share in
the news that the bones of their hero Levis had been
scattered and his aged widow and two daughters guillo-
tined? Adventuring children of the imposing France of
the kings—had not the old, uncoffined Louis the Great

himself planned their government?—sons and daughters of the royalist mood and the church, the Revolution struck at the very roots of their being. Few in
numbers and surrounded as they were, their core of
strength lay in the preservation of their identity, and
the fortress of their identity was their inheritance of
custom, language and religion. Only a very great and
confident nation may hazard the destruction of its past.

Abandoned by France as a government, and feeling in the influences of republican France a menace to their hopes of survival, they fell back upon themselves, looking within their hearts and to their own institutions for their strength. France, distant and alien, passed under a cloud. In January, 1810, a solemn Te Deum was chanted in the Catholic cathedral of Quebec for Nelson's victory of the Nile.

The new flag of France, the tricolor of the Revolution and Napoleon, was not, however, unknown upon the river. Travelers of the period mention seeing it now and then floating from the mastheads of French-Canadian boats. The name Napoleon, too, established itself in French-Canadian family life where it has lingered robustly to this day. Let Te Deums thunder as they would, the valley had its own pride in the Corsican ogre and his victories. A sound of Austerlitz and Wagram, of the feet of the Guard on the roads of Europe came echoing across the immensity of ocean, touching old loyalties and old prides remembered in the blood. But the psychic wound would not and did not heal: the two ways of life, the two moods, were never again to approach each other or even to run parallel. Great as it was, the physical and political separation was as nothing compared to this spiritual divorce. The French, on their side, would seem to have done little and cared less. To their nineteenth century indifference, Voltaire's "quelques arpents de neige" with its frozen rustics and feathered Indians had taken on something the quality of an old print folded into some dusty and neglected book once cherished, heaven knew why, by vanished generations. Neglected by literature and almost by history, the Canadian adventure, now passed under British rule, had only an antiquarian interest. A hundred years were to pass before France was to rediscover her colony in the beautiful and moving pages of *Maria Chapdelaine*.

A gulf of another kind stood between the conquered and the conquerors. The great portraits of the eighteenth century have preserved for us the military generation of the conquest, the wellborn young officers with their fine red coats, British high color and blue eyes who came sailing up the river at the end of summer burning the coasts and the harvests as they passed. Always a part of war, there are surely few things more hideous than the firing of the wheat. Military necessity or what you will, it is a positive act of death, a tragedy which offends both the ritual earth and the deepest instincts and values of our angry flesh and bone. Once victorious, what would these formidable milords do to the world of M. le Curé and his habitant congregation? In the years following the surrender, when life on the river stood still in an atmosphere of uncertainty and the wreckage of the past, a thought of the dispersion of the Acadians had haunted the valley with terror night and day. The conquered were only sixty thousand strong, and the same terrible policy might be followed on the river. Only when this first and elemental fear had died away had an understanding begun. The French had presently come to admit that the milords were not ogres. Murray had been their champion. Haldimand had ruled with very reasonable fairness, and parliamentary measures had been tolerant and conciliatory.

Measures had been urged against them which to this day provide a historic example of greed, injustice and brutality, but the crown itself had protected them from its own subjects. The Quebec act had guaranteed the Catholic religion and preserved to its clergy their customary powers and their tithes. The civil law had remained the law of France; only the criminal law had changed over to English usage, being considered more merciful than the French. There might be misgovernment, rapacity, racial contentions and all the familiar cynicism and absenteeism of the eighteenth century, but the elemental, the foundational rights were secure. The wind had been tempered to the shorn Canadian lamb. During the American Revolution, the people had in general favored the colonists and there had even been rebellious stirrings in the hearts of the younger clergy, but the higher clergy had kept discipline, preferring the Lion and the crown to all the siren twittering in the colonial bush.

From the uncertainty of such a past they had looked forward into an even more uncertain future. Isolated as human beings by their position in the valley and held there by the wilderness, isolated politically, religiously and racially, the world seemed to hold but a forlorn promise for their kind. Poor in the world's goods as they were, even tragically so, the only riches they could claim were such treasures as are laid up in heaven and the mystical intangibles of earth. They had nothing or they had all. They had their faith, they had their church, they had themselves and their simplicity and endurance, they had their past remembered and honored as a way of life; they had the cradle on rockers by the hearth. On earthly levels, the cradle carried the day. In the unhuman nights of wind and snow, in the winter moonlight of the spruces and the drifts, all up and down the valley small Henris and Pierres, small Joséphines and Maries came to help hold the land, card the wool, sow the wheat, and plough the furrow in the spring.

Early in the nineteenth century something began to emerge. It was at once an era and a way of life, a little civilization complete to the last gesture. Apparently as unknown as Paphlagonia or Crim Tartary to the large Jacksonian adventure over the border, it opposed the wide vigor, rascality, enterprise and roving unrest of the republic, a little hidden society founded upon established values and the religious spirit and living by popular custom and tradition. It was not an island of provincial France or a small French nation living in a Victorian mood under St. George's cross: like the Laurentian snows and the great cataracts, it was a thing in itself, an episode of the continent, "le vieux Canada", the golden age. Like an old room warmed by an open fire, the little society was warmed by that sense of human oneness and ultimate equality which the religious temper alone can give, and with this for its soul had retained traditional form and discipline. Neither the clergy nor the seigneurs had lost their prestige in the libertarian gusts of the American air. Confronted with the spectacle of other societies of European origin turning fluid as currents in a pool, the small obstinate nation on the St. Lawrence had made its adventure one of form and stability. Formlessness is a primordial quality or a part of death; it is the achieve-

ment of form which is life. Out of the many isolations
of the valley had emerged a homogeneous people sharing as one flesh and bone an unbroken continuity of
experience. Out of the undestroyed past had grown a
future. They had loved and honored their land and the
plough, and for all its winters and short summers it
had given them courage and strength. It was something that they were in no danger of finding life too
easy. The village steeple, through everything, had been
nothing less than the Rock of Ages. The cradle was
saying nothing but keeping continuously at work. They
were not crowded, they were growing, and their struggle with nature had the satisfactions of the victor.
Whatever it was, the effort was not a war on life.

The great stream had created something unique.
On its green and northern banks it presented to history
a long mid-nineteenth century idyll of earth and man,
an eclogue among the spruce of labor, endurance and
content. No far sound of the rowdy high spirits over the
border came to trouble it; no sound of its village mills
traveled across the mountains to alarm the apprehen-
sive New England ear. The wars were over and done.
In all North American history there had been only one
such unified, complete and picturesque adventure in
living. Between the eighteenth century and the hideous
industrial perversion "le vieux Canada" stands as a kind
of triumph, unpretending and patient, of the mystery
of the spirit of man, its sleigh bells ringing on the winter air, and the songs of its woodsmen rising from the
sudden descents and encirclements of fog which in
summer hide sun and shore from the midstream passage of the river.

II

The British officers of the town garrisons began at once to make themselves at home. Stationed in the evergreen north of the savage (and to them almost bearish) new world and up to their noses in winter snow, they soon invented an Anglo-Canadian social life to go with the climate and the country. It became a world of sleighing parties, picnics, visits to waterfalls, and excursions over the ice to favorite Canadian inns. The British officer of the late eighteenth century and the early nineteenth was no redcoat dullard. On the contrary, he was most often a very civilized and pleasant youngster, one no more afraid of showing his skill as a water-colorist than he was of his ability as a marksman, and quite ready, as Wolfe was, to quote a fine line at some crisis of his life. He had a taste for nature, too; grandiose, perhaps, and a little rhetorical, yet entirely genuine and deeply felt. A great Laurentian cataract among the spruces and the black preadamite cliffs stirred his imagination. One sees him in that distant past, a figure with flaxen hair and blue eyes wearing traveling dress and seated before an easel placed a comfortable distance from the spray. All over Canada you find them, these little excellent water colors, ancestral and military; and sometimes there is a miniature of the young man himself, wearing his British Majesty's red and gold.

The short summer passed as it would, no more bringing the Iroquois, but continuing with the eternal American mosquito. After the pleasure of the change, colonels and captains, majors and majors' daughters, all the garrison masculine and feminine turned in their hearts toward the winter. In summer the roads were the most primitive of tracks; one could scarce budge from the already bad roads of the towns, but with ice and snow came freedom, gaiety and speed. Then out came the great sleighs, some painted gaily in French eighteenth century fashion with flowers and playful scrolls, others all a bright color of huntsman red. Out came the fine strong horses, out came the fur robes, and the fur mittens and the great fur hats, and the real fun began. Cleared of its wayward fog and its summer uncertainties of rain, the Canadian sky mingled its threatening snow-cloud forms with a North American splendor of winter blue, the river itself turning to a greenish boulevard of ice. Earth no longer, but mountain shapes of pure snow unbroken and white from crest to crest, the Laurentians rose beyond the snow-covered farms and houses to the ever empty and arctic sky. There was visiting and calling on friends, the keen sound of sleigh bells growing fainter after the good-byes smothered in furs, the painted sleigh speeding along the frozen river and disappearing a point of motion in a great panorama of sky and snow.

Young officers from London tried out their snow-shoes on the Plains of Abraham; there were toboggan parties and hunting parties and expeditions to Lorette where the Indians heightened the picturesque and there was a comfortable inn. The favorite promenade of the officers and their ladies was to the Falls of Montmorency. It was something of an adventure then for sleighs could get lost between Quebec and the cataract when mounds and drifts had obscured the tracks of the

runners and twilight had fallen on the river. But forth
they went, making up parties as garrisons do the world
over, bundling the ladies in carefully and putting in a
heated stone or a fine hot stick of birch for their feet
to rest on under the mountainous robes. Then the cataract in its eighteenth century beauty and unspoiledness
pouring its ivory splendor between the whiter snow
and the black, adamantine cliff, all seen with the eight-

JE SVIS VN CHIEN QVI RONGE LO
EN LE RONGEANT JE PREND MON REPOS
VN TEMS VIENDRA QVI NESTPAS VENV
QVI JE MORDERAY QVIMAVRA MORDV

eenth century eye. In some sheltered nook of the cliffs
whirled and towered the smoke of the welcome, the
life-giving fire. One hears the sound of the fall, the
English voices, the bells of the sleighs, and the winter
eeriness of the wind's cry above the miles of ice. As
the gathering returned to Quebec in the dusk, they
could see the lights of the French farmhouses standing
far up above the river on the slopes.

It is all far away now, but it was the little and
the great adventure of its time. The artists painted it
again and again, and the young men who could draw

entered it in their sketchbooks, putting their gloves back on their numbed fingers. Later on, perhaps by some winter voyage from Halifax, a sketch and a letter would go to some house in Scotland or the foggy Midlands, and there would be a thought of Canada and of the new country and the different way of life.

III

In the fine old house which Governor Haldimand had built at the Falls of Montmorency, lived the most notable member of the British garrison. To this day, his name remains alive in Canada, having become a part of the picturesqueness of Laurentian history. This was Prince Edward of Kent and Strathern, fourth son of King George III, later to be famous as the father of Queen Victoria. Prince Edward of Kent (he was not yet the "Duke": this was to come later) had arrived in Canada on August 11, 1791, in command of the Seventh Fusiliers. Born in 1767, he was then a personable young Hanoverian of twenty-four. The prince had not arrived alone. The pleasant country house presented a scene of domesticity and exemplary decorum which was all the more human and touching for being entirely irregular. Edward had brought with him his discreet and amiable mistress named—and the name must have been chosen by the Muse of History—the Baroness Saint-Laurent.

They were both young, both of the same age, and the domesticity had begun at twenty-three. The British took it all very calmly, royal irregularities being a his-

torical and consistent part of the drama of thrones.
Mr. Huckleberry Finn, explaining to Jim the picturesque lapses of crowned hearts, would seem to have
had something of the same attitude, though expressed
with more human pride. The French understood completely. In such cases they have always been moved
far more by the values of good breeding and the social
virtues displayed than by the moral mechanics of the
law. The baroness was a Frenchwoman of their own
ancestral land, pretty, young, unmistakably of good
family, and with a charming gift of courtesy. Men-
tioning "le Prince Édouard" in their letters, they called
the baroness "sa digne et aimable compagne". There
could be no higher praise. They saw her in her furs
driving with her prince down the old French streets,
or walking, attended by some woman companion, along
the great platform of the old French fortifications.
The couple seem to have gone together to Niagara. Edward was in Canada from 1791 to 1794, and from
1795 to 1798. The intervening period he had spent sol-
diering with the expedition of Sir Charles Grey against
the French West India Islands. "Madame St. Laurent
has been with me in all climates" said Edward later to
the diarist, Mr. Creevy.

The quasi marriage was to last twenty-seven years.
It was brought to an end by the duke's sense of duty
to the crown of Britain and the royal family. There
were no heirs. "Although," he said, again to Creevy, "I
trust I shall be at all times ready to obey any call my
country might make upon me, God only knows the
sacrifice it will be to make it whenever I shall think it
my duty to become a married man." Whatever hap-

pened, Madame Saint Laurent must be given an annuity secured for life sufficient to keep up a suitable establishment and a carriage. The duke had the carriage much upon his mind, and came back to it on various occasions. No, it was not going to be easy to desert his old friend and companion. "Think of Mrs. Creevy, Mr. Creevy!" The baroness, getting wind of what was going on, had hysterics at the breakfast table. But hysterics were nothing to the awesome demands of the crown. Leave the lady, he did, and on May 29, 1818, married with all civil and ecclesiastical propriety the Princess Victoria of Saxe-Coburg. On May 24, 1819, arrived at Kensington Palace the child who was to be the future queen.

The Duke of Kent died the very next year, having got wet through in a cold Devonshire rain. History has been not overkind to the duke. He is remembered as an officer so absurdly meticulous in regard to everything properly military, that Wellington and the army called him "The Corporal". And there is something both absurd and painful in his desertion of his partner and his sudden and dutiful high-mindedness towards the future of the crown. But he had his points. The separation was not cold-blooded, as separations in such circumstances have often been, and he fought like a lion for the carriage. He stood out, moreover, for Catholic emancipation and was a member of the Anti-Slavery Society, the Bible Society, and the Society for Promoting Christianity Among the Jews. With the Coburg marriage, Mme. Saint-Laurent, too, disappears. Perhaps she retired to Brussels or Restoration France, perhaps to some town in England such as Bath, for she had made her life in an English atmosphere. One can be sure there was nothing of Becky Sharp. But it is not to these later years (whose history must remain conjectural) that the imagination returns, but to youth and the Canadian adventure. The lady is remembered on the St. Lawrence: she was very much part of her time. The houses she occupied are still to be seen, one in Quebec city, the other by the falls. Both dwellings have been knocked about, and the second has been changed to some degree outside and in, but it is not difficult to see what it must have been during Prince Edward's tenancy. The lady would have had a chamber on the east overlooking the superb cataract. The afternoon sun falls directly upon its plunging wreaths and tresses, slanting away at sundown with a last and northern glow. One thinks of her, the young and pretty Frenchwoman, a wife by temperament and circumstance, standing at the Georgian window in the thick Canadian wall. The room darkens and the fall is seen no more, nothing remaining but the mystery of trees and the cataract sound rising and falling, becoming lost and returning in the cold oncoming of the huge Laurentian night.

IV

It was the Romantic age which must be seen a little in its own genteel and agreeable gleam. British officers and Canadian seigneurs, Indians and traders, habitants and voyageurs, the drums of Napoleon roll behind them in the picture, and presently sounding their last flourish, hang silent as trophies on a wall. It was to the age which followed, the age of Byron and Scott, that the remote French province presently attached itself, returning to the course of history. Having refused the Revolution, it accepted the era of decorum, bowing to it with its own old-fashioned courtesy in outward things. The old portraits on the river, even as they are in Quebec, are oftenest of the Ingres world. The fine eyes look down at us from beneath the arranged and heavy ringlets, the vast bonnet hanging ready to be worn above the tight bodice and the silken balloonings of the sleeves. The men stare out meditative, assured in money and the things of the world, perhaps less certain of the new direction of life. Ingres vanishes, and the years belong to Winterhalter; and presently it is the world of Victoria and Albert at Balmoral with Bertie at their feet. On the river, too, there is change. But the time is not the time of a world rushing with complacency across the nineteenth century. By the St. Lawrence it is the earth's time, and the wheat's time and the time of the curé and the seigneur and the peaceful flowing of the days.

v

The last of the snow melted from the roofs, and pitched with a roar over the eaves, the great patches of snow grew smaller on the hills; on the river the ice floes shrank under the longer day and the long glance of the sun. Travelers along the coastal road heard the cataracts of the mountains roaring inland behind the screens of spruce, the sound mingling with the wind. The smell of snow was going out of the world; the smell of water and colder earth was again part of the air.

With the increasing warmth and the first of summer began the earth-ritual of the wheat. The growing of an Indian corn is an adventure on the lower river, a kind of annual hope which either quickens to a chance success or dies away to little or nothing in the rain. It was the wheat, the ancient wheat of Europe and the ancestral past, the spiked plant of the Osirian Nile, of the threshing floors of the Philistines, of the Roman villas of Gaul and the medieval granaries which was to be depended upon, and was very life for all along the stream. Being life, it was a part of the religious mood and the divine mystery, a seed to be sown with a prayer in a first furrow opened with a prayer. Isis was no more, nor Ceres, the ancient mothers of the field, but in their place stood the Virgin of the Laurentians with her choir of saints, gathering both the sheaf and the human soul into the shelter of her earthly tenderness and divine compassion. Up and down the chosen field, flinging the seed from the bag slung at his side, walking the dark earth and making with every stride the most beautiful and poignant of all human gestures, walked in the morning each good man of the river, each father of a family, archpriests in homespun of the wheat and the St. Lawrence. Presently the grain stirred. Challenging the crest of the forests to the north, the emerging multitude of spears colored the hills with their delicate yet austere mystery of green. Growing faster with its gaining strength, thrusting out of the earth in the cool Laurentian night, forming its noble and hieratic blade under August sunlight and the great fantastic clouds, the plant ripened, turned to gold, and was ready for the long hours of the reaping. It was no feast of machines. The reaping of the golden age was done by hand, the reapers bending over with their sickles as one sees them in medieval books of hours. It was thought unseemly to force the speed of the cutting; some instinct, profoundly wise, warned them not to destroy the religious mood and pattern

with haste and ugliness. The work was hard. Back and arms grew wrenched from stooping and striking, the ripened heads scattered their chaff and barbs, but gather by gather the sheaves thickened and rounded, and sickle by sickle life itself was gathered from the earth.

The young and the old of every house, all the family from great-grandparents down to small children scarce uncradled, came to the reaping. The hillsides were aswarm. At noon there was singing all up and down the slopes. A young man sang, and his song was taken up by others; choral ballads and choral refrains came choiring over the meat and bread, and this would be followed by silence and the rustle of the wheat and the sigh of wind till a song began again. Songs and the mood were merry. Days later, after the threshing and more hard work, the yield rolled off to the community mill to be ground by some mountain stream into good and honest flour. "The first duty of a Canadian seigneur," said the old royal law, "shall be the building of a mill." The folk of the golden age did not suffer, as we do, from that bleached and lifeless dust which is our flour or that sweet and lifeless ghost which is our bread. Their wheat gave them blood and bone. The rich, living grain made them rugged and enduring, a hardy people going about their tasks and asking no favors from the northwest wind. Driving their canoes through rapids, swinging the ax in the deep snow of the woods, ploughing and reaping, their own hillsides gave strength to strength. In the level country there was wheat to sell. From one parish alone on the Richelieu five hundred thousand bushels went out each year to the cities.

The wheat had been sown, reaped, and stored, the oats and the barley gathered, the potatoes, apples, and cabbages husbanded; let winter come, there would be life in the houses and the barns. The ritual of earth and human life had been again rehearsed on the familiar altar of the year. To quote the poignant phrase of Antigone, "It is eternal, and no man knows whence it came."

VI

Among the farms there was very little, almost piti-
fully little, in the way of things and possessions. Old
and smoke-blackened boxes of birchbark, both shape
and manner of making borrowed from the Montagnais,
could hold the pepper and salt: the coarse, strong blankets had as little of creature-comfort as a board. A
New England farmer's house with its comfortable furniture, its Georgian inheritances, its flowered teapots
and cups from Staffordshire and its papered walls and
Currier prints would have seemed by comparison a
lodge in an English park. If a morsel of ancestral furniture existed, it was usually some great farm cupboard,
an "armoire" with paneled doors of French eighteenth
century design. These passed from eldest son to eldest
son together with the cradle and the family crucifix.
Agricultural implements were hereditary even as they
had been in the France of the kings. Were a new sickle
needed in the wheat, it was hammered at the village
forge from any suitable steel which could be found;
perhaps from some old pike or blade used long ago
against the Iroquois.

What then were the possessions of "les anciens" of
the golden age? In the handsome old-fashioned houses
of the towns, with their formal French masonry and
roofs of slate, in the unpainted, snow-heaped wooden
cottages of the wilder parishes, what of the temporal
and invisible and timeless was cherished by the human
spirit? Their religion stood first. It gave focus and a
meaning to their lives, gathering into its ancestral and
familiar piety their whole world from the farmer and

his family driving to mass to the young coureur de bois
saying an Ave by his solitary fire. It is to be noted that
the religion was not then so rigidly institutionalized.
With religion and the religious mood, perhaps a part of
the same region of "Mansoul", was the sense of peasant content and oneness with the earth. What may be
called Anglo-Saxon America has known little of this
rustic and poignant unity. The land is used and ever has
been used as one might use a tractor, but it is not loved
to the bone. Yet in England it is so loved, loved to
heartbreaking with an inarticulate devotion. Some hidden quality of poetic emotion has vanished here, dying
of a sea change. The Canadian of the river, for all his
redoubtable prowess with the ax, was at peace with his
earth and his fields. Ploughing, sowing, reaping, he made
his "terres" part of his humanity even as it had been
part of the humanity of others. Where generation follows generation upon an ancestral earth, and fathers
and sons, and sons who are to be, plough the same hill,
a field becomes a mystical as well as a material inheritance. One possesses and is in turn possessed. His valley
was northern and short of summer, but the earth was
"good"; the plough had its reward. The lower valley,
too, had remained French and their very own. From the
northern lights glowing, vanishing and reappearing
above the arctic wilderness it was theirs south across the
great St. Lawrence to the wild frontier of Maine. Peace
dwelt on the stream, and there was assurance of possession and the permanence of blood, and an accompanying mood of permanence. Higher up the hills, eastward toward the sea, and inland along the tributaries

plenty of land awaited the surplus many. The satisfactions of earth were joined to the hopes of heaven.

I have left to the last the possession which to all observers of the time seemed particularly characteristic of the race. It was social gaiety. That one source of the high spirits was the French temperament is undeniable, though France and French life, either reflected in literature or observed, are not really gay. There is nothing gay in the literary picture of mid-nineteenth century peasant life with its terrible rot of avarice and its clumsy but profoundly-willed cunning forever up to mischief. Ironic and intellectual humor there is, with its sharp fun or Latin urbanity, and a kind of larking frivolity which can be curiously without merriment, but true gaiety is seldom of the picture. In historic reality, the gaiety of French Canada and the old-fashioned Canadian was a last fortress and outpost of a forsaken mood of the human spirit. It was more than a reflection of temperament or race. What had lived on beside the river was something of the vanished mood of which "Merrie England" had been once a part, the mood which had somehow shriveled in the fierce controversies of the Reformation, and died back into the earth at the French Revolution. It was spiritually a part of the world of Breughel and his peasant feasts and skating parties, a link with the country musicians of Teniers, and the masked dancers of the English shires. Of the world in which Goldsmith could wander indolently over Europe earning his bread by playing on a flute, it was the last light to be seen, its final bow to history.

As a little world and a little nation, the golden age of "les anciens" is no more. The festival of the wheat is almost at an end. As a way of life, however, and as a mood, the age has not died. Strong outposts remain, and manners and customs then established are powerful in the French community. Encountering the enchantments of progress, it has modified itself, adjusting itself to the chaos as best it can. Here it has succumbed or retreated, here it has made its compromise, here it has accepted the change as one might take a recommended but unpalatable dose. Beyond the industrialism of the smaller towns, raw, inchoate, and of an ugliness almost without parallel, it lives by a relation to the soil. The little farm one passes on the road, unspoiled in its ancient greenery, is part of it; the woman plying her spinning wheel at the lonely house is its daughter; the hardy, patient, crowded-out young men gathering at the communion rail in the chapel of the lumber camp are its disinherited sons. Let it be noted that the time of "les anciens" was not Utopia. Many things had remained too primitive, there was little intellectual life, and saving popular song and music, little art of any kind. There were rough places on its road, and its first contact with the new "Captains-of-Industry" world introduced its simple and kindly people to a particularly cruel and unfeeling exploitation. But it was human of the blood and human of the pattern, friendly of spirit, thoroughly alive, and profoundly at peace with its earth. As a venture in human living, it is not without its small nobility. It lives on, no ghost, because its values live, and these, I think, will not die till a last Ave is said at the ploughing, and the last of the great mill wheels, ceasing its noble thundering and plashing, stops forever on its Laurentian hill.

2
Montreal to Quebec

I т is the light of earliest morning, the sun being scarce an hour high, and the ships which have been moving up the river in the night are entering the port of Montreal. One by one they come, neat freighters of the new dispensation, very trim of paint and bright work in the freshened light and air, each with its national flag flying heraldic at the stern. Pointed like fingers against them, the red spar buoys of the channel slant with the current to the east, bobbing and dipping and rolling about in the great seaward rush of the navigable stream. The city lies to the north, a modern port of business streets and wharves backed by a forest hill which might have been discovered yesterday. With its isolate shapes of mountains to the south, blue mountains of the border wilderness as remote in mood from the city as an Indian grave in the woods, the port has something of an unreal air in this North American space: a second glance might not find it under this red Indian and archaic sky.

Ships approaching from the Lakes are hidden in the huge country to the west. Dropping down out of the canals, facing into this early sun, they are leaving behind the sound of the rapids, and drawing near the noise of the water front and the city.

Eastward, now, lies that reach of the river which is forever the river of New France, that great St. Lawrence stream whose banks seemed almost one French village from Quebec to Montreal in the eyes of eighteenth century observers. One glides first into a quiet of rural scenes, the Bay of Montreal narrowing into a passage through les Îles Verchères. These are small islands flat as meadows and as green, each larger being occupied by one comfortable French farm with its barns and gardens, its house maples and pasture elms, and its horses and cows who scarce bother to look when ships slide past. So full of swallows' nests are the low and gravelly banks that the traveler may here look down on the pretty sight of bank swallows behaving quite like sea birds, their dark and graceful shapes skimming beside the ship in level and accompanying flight. The kildeer, too, is a lover of these isles, flying off with cries when the cattle tread too near or move to the riverbank to drink.

East of these farms, a fine channel leads uninterrupted on to the Lac St. Pierre. The country is a glaciated flatness, the valley floor lying wide and level to each side. To the north are farms and villages lost a little in the vagueness, and a nearer glimpse of an old river road and its towns; to the south stands a parallel road, houses and farms and towns with red-brick buildings screened in branches, and views of spires far away beyond a belt of trees. Almost everywhere a part of the landscape, the serried towers of high-tension electricity radiate out of the cold space and void to the north carrying power down from the cataracts, and disappearing like Martians into some pale nowhere of this vast regional scale.

Nearer at hand, navigation marks, range lights and aviation towers straddle up above quiet orchards and pastures by the bank, with official freshness of paint reflecting the northern sun.

Another barrier of farm and meadow islands (les Îles Sorel), islands large as prairie townships and as flat, another passing of rich farms each with its own boats and market scows, and one ventures forth upon the inland sea of the Lac St. Pierre. French-Canadian folk-lore and song have much to say of this lake famous for its lumber rafts and lumbermen of an older day, and for the ever-capricious storms and gales which burst upon its shallows. Today the ships come and go across its flatness, trailing their plumes of smoke along its level sky, freighters, tankers, government tenders and small liners following the buoyed channel for thirty miles on one great line.

It is here, by this blue widening of the river which was once a much greater glacial sea, that the earliest French explorers, coming from the east, must have had their first sense and emotion of America as a continent. These levels and distances, this paler sky, are the first of the inland west; this blue water is in aspect and mood a first of the Great Lakes. An end has come to the bold adventure of the sea so far west into the earth; here is the assertion of another scale and another integrity with other clouds and powers.

Changing back again from a lake to a river, the stream presently brings the traveler to the important industrial town of Trois Rivières. Here the old French heritage has coalesced with an industrial modernity careless and huge as that to the south of the border; even the vast natural presence of the river becoming for a moment scummed with man. A ferry churns across to a greener southern bank; a choking foulness of sulphur and pulp from the paper mills hangs in the air. Pale and cold with wilderness mud, a great tributary, the St. Maurice, here ends its long journey down from the forest savagery above.

Two great forces, one human and of the spirit, one natural and of the earth, have set their seal upon the noble reach ahead. The first is the influence of Quebec, of that Quebec which is more than a visible city, being a fortress of a way of life, the citadel of an ancestral past whose flag has never been lowered from its staff. More and more now, standing closer to these unseen and spiritual walls, the old parishes to each bank strengthen into the mood of France, each hamlet gathered about the sword of some central and Catholic spire. The other force is the descent and approach of the northern forest to the narrowing region of the river. A vast and unhuman savagery of trees and mountains, the plough has long cleared it from the bank, but it has never made peace, being too great in itself and timeless to change in elemental mood. Back of the river, a sparse scatter of hamlets thins in a few hacked miles to an end, the roads come to an end, and nothing lies ahead but a great anonymity and implacability of green. It is this forest which sweeps across the French-Canadian imagination even as the northern lights sweep the forest itself glowing above its solitudes and desolations.

Making no great turns but rather swaying or inclining for long miles now to the north of east, now more to its south, the St. Lawrence streams on towards the still far distant sea. The flat country is falling behind, the western mood vanishing from earth and sky. This is the east again, the clearings and the trees. To the south, towns, farms, churches, and ecclesiastical establishments come one after another into view, all standing a little back from the river and seemingly below the local boldness of shore like seventeenth century cities behind their level fortifications. To the north, the hamlets are now on the shore line, now above on the shoulders of the hills.

Mile by mile, the river in its swiftness, in its great outpouring, is entering a passage leading to the narrows of Quebec. Something like a great trench is opening ahead. It has for walls, the woodland that was once a forest, and the stream is flowing direct and strong between its darknesses of green. From these brown, these muddied eddies twisting past, these taut glistenings and speedings without foam, the color borrowed from the wider sky has gone: the river now is all the earth's. Ships pass in the enclosed serenity with the directness of vessels in deep waters: a churning sound of water, a quiet heartbeat of engines and they are gone. On river-level tracks to the north a train appears and disappears as in a film, an old village slides sideways out of a cove, a lovely spire of eighteenth century stone is seen for a long moment under a hill, else all is old and of the woods and of the mood of the woods. The activities of man have fallen back to the higher and more level land above these green descents.

The walls are rising as one draws near Quebec. Approaching the city a sky line of ragged trees high to the north, might be a sky line in the deep north woods, yet the tracks are at its base and the ships are never far. The sun has long ago crossed the river to the sky on the northern side. It is a northern sun now in a northern sky, with a new silveriness looking down to northern seas and forest solitudes. A great sweep of the stream and the bridge appears in its more than human scale; a bar of shadow across the waters, and it is gone. Trees are giving way to cleared land and the waterside huddle of modernity. Another turn, and the towering ridge of wilderness rock which is the ark of Quebec is swelling out from the north to narrow the channel and force the St. Lawrence through its gates. Here is Wolfe's Cove with its fatal path to the plains above, here the Gibraltar rock of the citadel with its crevices of weed and its Victorian parapets above, here the waterside road where the colonials were held on the long-ago December night while volleys crashed between the dark of the river and the cliffside pale with snow.

The walls approach; the ferries passing and repassing between of the foot of Levis cliff and the Quebec landing, falling off seaward as they start with the greater rush of the stream. A long thrust, and the river has passed in its immensity of will, pouring its muddied stream past the docks, the liners, and the guns out into the sudden, the magical and the sealike enlargement of the leagues of Quebec Bay.

A reflection of blue lies on the water ahead. Sea gulls fly and soar about the ships as they come into view, turning the Isle of Orleans, and there are tidal stains on the piers, yet this is not the sea. These eddies, these muddied, back-up tides are fresh: a hundred miles to the eastward cattle will come to drink of them as they pass eddying. The great river is still master of its own.

CHAPTER SEVEN

Legends for a Winter Night

WHAT a national folklore most importantly reveals is a nation's sense of beauty and wonder. Its way of life, its quids and quiddities of character, its essential values and its beliefs—these can be found well enough in its history and its more formal literature, but the poetic spirit in the popular soul can only reveal itself in a literature of popular inspiration. In such a mirror, in such a pool of legend and myth what is seemingly timeless in a people confronts what is timeless and of mystery in their world. The past, when it is seen, is never the past of books, but the past of popular emotion and poetic feeling; four walls never seem to enclose it and its action takes place under the sky. Beneath the field the young men who have died in battle sing their farewell, and mingle with the wind their lament and their pride.

The songs of the French Canadian, as I have written in another chapter, are lyrics in form and mood. The ballad, though it exists, has much less importance both as folklore and as song. Long lugubrious narratives such as delight the western cowboy were never a real part of the customs of New France. You will not hear any "Lord Rendal" sung by these hearths. When there was a story to tell, the French spirit gave it over to prose, in this manner bringing into being a whole body of narrative legend which is unique in the New World. Indeed the only parallels to the stories one hears at a campfire in the bush are the fabliaux of the Middle Ages. The French-Canadian world, however, is a world far more primitive and mysterious than the old France of castles and Reynard the Fox. The forest of the north is part of it, and the blue, empty mountains which carry the land to the desolation of the eternal fogs; the beaver and the otter and the wolf are there and the Indian and his ghosts. Upon its paths a folk tale which might have come from the brothers Grimm can turn a corner of the spirit and seem like something its narrator overheard when last among the Crees. Other tales, other versions, remain complete old France. The familiar tale of the priest who returned as a spirit to finish a mass said too hastily is a legend told from one end of Catholic Europe to the other: in French Canada it is told of some parish at Sorel. Many of the tales are Breton in their origins. The campfire crackles, the tea pail boils, the immense night waits beyond the small immediate world of trees and the fire, and as one listens the Breton imagination creates its world in the American forest, dissolving the wilderness itself into a moment's unsubstantiality, and evoking in its place the moors, the sound below of the grey Breton sea, and the long ranks and solitary avenues of the evil, pagan and immemorial stones.

Of the four legends I have here set down, three appear in print for the first time. These are "The Haycocks of Le Très Fort", "The Wolf of l'Échafaud des Basques" and "The Fiddler of the Northern Lights". I set down "The Haycocks" first because it is the most

Breton in its mood. No exact parallel to it seems to exist in Breton folklore though there are many tales which bear it a close resemblance. I have chosen the second tale because it mingles the French-Canadian imagination with something seemingly Indian. The werewolf of its narrative is clearly not the bloody-mouthed horror which perhaps more than any other

single invention haunts the folklore of medieval France; he is an Algonquin spirit. In the world of the French mind, it is horrible that a human being should ever change into a beast: in the Algonquin mind such a change is a part of things, expected, and even casual, as it is here. The wolf on the floe, moreover, is beast in shape rather than beast in spirit, and though he inspires fear, he never becomes the figure of rending terror who follows on the moonlit path across the high uplands of Auvergne. The legend of Cadieu is probably some historical incident which has been kept alive as popular poetry. A number of versions exist, some of them so vague and worthless that it is impossible to tell what happened, and one has to search among many renderings to restore coherency to the narrative. The song the coureur de bois is said to have left behind—it is variously called "La Complainte de Cadieu" or "Petit Rocher de la Haute Montagne"—may possibly have certain early origins or be essentially a later song of the voyageurs, the version current today being unmistakably early nineteenth century in diction. It is to be noted that the song and the various tales about the song are a little at odds as to exactly what happened. Whatever did occur, the crux of the action was certainly the situation at the portage, and the attempt of Cadieu to save his wife and his companions by luring away the Iroquois.

I am adding "The Fiddler of the Northern Lights" because it is in its essence something very French-Canadian. For other folk tales of the northern lights one has to go to the literature of Finland and Scandinavia, particularly to the first, discovering there that world of magicians and incantations which is the ghost of the old shamanism of the Asiatic past. The magical drum sings, the ancient, white-bearded wizard shouts and calls upon the powers, and the great lights of the north shake and ripple above the terror of the spells. The more familiar European literature is silent. Though it may be seen above Norman farms and the towers of Chartres, the aurora is there never a background of

human action as it is here, night after burning night. In
the present story one is in Canada and nowhere else.
It is against the Canadian forest and its sky that the
fiddler moves, the roar of the St. Maurice sounding in
his ears, and a beginning glow of the aurora gathering
like a pale web of light across the stars. And the fiddler,
who is he? There is something in him akin to those
wandering figures to whom the years cannot bring
death, who by land and sea haunt the human imagination, but he is an habitant as well, even such a one as
might be on his way home from midnight mass on
Christmas Eve. He has taken a strange path, yet it may
be that he will hear again the sacring bell. As the curé
says, "all things are possible to God."

The Haycocks of Le Très Fort

On the south shore of the St. Lawrence long miles
of level meadows lie between the river and the road,
the blue domes and mounds of the Laurentians gazing
across to them over the wide and intervening stream.
The native sparrows who have a liking for the coast
know well these shores and meadows, whirring up from
the pale grass to take refuge by bush or fence when
startled, only to descend again with another rush of
small wings when the fear has passed, and in the late
summer and the autumn the clear whistle of the visiting yellowlegs—le chevalier aux pieds jaunes—comes
with its poignant sweetness from the borders of the
tides. When the evening Angelus has been rung, it is
the heron who breaks from the darkness before the
solitary walker, a great shape struggling to clear the

earth, attaining and circling off, and disappearing with a harsh croak of protest overhead. Far down the stream the winking lights of buoys give distance to a world else become invisible, a world else withdrawn into a lonely imemnsity of peace.

In one region the meadows and marshes are scattered over with great boulders deeply embedded in the shore. The river here sweeps close, and the blackish and rounded bulks of stone stand in their haphazard congregations against the coiling alongshore streams and the far vistas and the widening distances.

The people of a neighboring village, it is said, once held in common the meadows of salt hay. It was the custom for the village to go together to the mowing, each household cutting and gathering its own share, and tossing and spreading out the fallen grass while the Norman scythes worked busily ahead. The hay thus cut, however, did not all find a rightful shelter in its owner's barn. A villager of giant size and strength, whom the others called "le très fort" had a way of taking the hay of others and adding it to his own. So afraid were they all of the strength and formidable manner of this terrifying solitary that little could be done about the pillage. Taking what he would and from whom he would, the strong man was lord of the hay, and his fellow villagers were as nothing before his authority of fear.

After some years of this robbery and injustice, the villagers gave up their rights, and staying at home enlarged the pastures and hayfields about their farms. Only a poor widow and her daughter who had almost no land at all remained to share the marsh hay with le très fort.

One fine summer morning, they say, the two women went to the meadows to cut and gather their yearly share. Both were hard workers and as they raked and mowed, friendly neighbors came to them across the fields to lend a helping hand. By noon their little portion had been cut and spread to cure in the hot sun. Leaving the grass to season, the women returned to the village and their house.

Late in the afternoon they went again to the meadows to rake the hay into hills. As they turned the corner of a wall and came in sight of the river they saw someone working in the meadows they had left and in their own small corner of the hay. It was le très fort who had spent the afternoon mowing, and was now raking all the hay in sight into hills of his own. Approaching him with fear in their hearts, the women ventured to protest.

"Monsieur," said the poor mother timidly, "that is our hay."

"All the hay is mine," replied le très fort.

"But our cow cannot live without our hay," protested the girl.

This time le très fort made no reply, but went on raking as if he had heard nothing and there were no one near.

"What does he care if we all die?" said the mother. "Come, daughter, we can only pray."

Returning with heavy hearts through the approach of sundown, the two women knelt by a roadside across, and implored Heaven for justice and aid. That

evening the villagers saw le très fort working late into
the dusk, tossing up and brandishing great forkfuls of
hay with a fury and a tirelessness which seemed to them
to have little in it of the human. None saw him or heard
him returning in the dark. Sometime soon after midnight there was a moment of rain, whisper, a sound in
the night, and all again was still.

When the sun rose on another fine day, a confused
sound of voices, a growing and excited murmur began
to fill the streets between the gabled roofs. Soon everybody was hurrying out of doors, putting on their coats
as they came. At the end of the street those who lived in
view of the river were gathered in front of their houses
calling on their neighbors to look at the wonder in the
meadows. The haycocks of le très fort had been every
one of them turned to stone! Only the haycocks made
of the widow's hay had been spared, and there they
were, tall and sweet, with the new boulders ringed
about them. Nobody ever again saw le très fort. Some
think he is one of the stones.

Those who live near say that the great autumnal
tides sweep in among the boulders with a roar and a
crying which is like no other sound on all the coast.

THE WOLF OF L'ÉCHAFAUD DES BASQUES

"When my grandfather was a little boy, he heard
a story about a loup-garou. In those days, the story was
one told among the elders when the children had gone
to bed, but one night my grandfather was wakeful, and
overheard the *récit* as I am telling it to you. It was an
old story then, so the thing itself must have happened

a long, long time ago, in the ancient days of the sailing ships and the voyageurs.

"Somewhere on the river near l'Échafaud des Basques, in that country of wild rocks and shallow coves and the winter ice, there was a house of fisherfolk and hunters. One night in the earliest spring, a night of the full moon, they heard and then heard again a strange sound of cries coming from the river. The lumber people had not then cut the timber of the coast, so the country was forest and not bush, and the people in the hut at first imagined they were hearing the outcries of an animal. The ice was still in the fleuve, a wilderness of floes sailing to and fro with the tides as far as the eye could see: what would a human being be doing in such a place? But now they heard the cries again. Two young men went out and saw by the moonlight what seemed to be the figure of a man lying on a floe drifting past the opening of their cove and as they gazed, the figure raised itself and cried to them for help. Their boats had been covered over with evergreen branches and were buried in ice and snow, but they dug one out, all the people of the hut helping and working very fast, and at great peril to themselves the young men put out and rescued the man from the river and the ice.

"It was a young man dressed in the strong warm clothes of the people of the coast. When they carried him into the hut, they saw that he had brown hair and very strange grey eyes. We are a hardy people, but even les anciens were surprised to find that he had not frozen a cheek or his fingers and toes though he had been two days and a night upon the river. He told them that he came from a settlement many miles to the east, and that he had been trying to cross over to an island when the ice opened and carried him away.

"In those days, people came and went, especially the young men, with the freedom of birds, so it did not seem strange to the fisher people when the young man settled down among them, and made no effort to return to the place whence he had come. He was wiry, quick, and strong, and they were glad of his aid. For a part of the summer he went to work with a family who were making a clearing in the woods. There was a pretty girl in the neighborhood, one of a large family: her name was Laure-Louise. Her father was one of those making land. They were good people, but like all the people on that coast in those days, simple and without money. Believing that the young man would make a good husband, they made no objection when he came to their house to court one of their daughters.

"So it went on all the late summer, and on through the autumn and the winter into the beginning of the spring.

"The year had turned the long corner, but there was still snow on the ground and the ice was still in the river. One evening the older brother of Laure-Louise—he was named Bernadin—decided to drive over to the house where the other young man was staying with the people he had been helping. Bernadin had business with the people of the house, not with the young man, so he invited Laure-Louise to come with him. While her brother and the people of the house were talking, Laure-Louise and the young man talked by themselves. The young man seemed very restless and uneasy, acting so strangely that Laure-Louise could make nothing of him, and going over to her brother asked to be taken home. It was the spring, and something of a warmish wind was blowing over the forest and the softening snow. The moon was a few days old and was still high for they were returning in good season. At a dark place in the road the horse gave a sudden start, and broke into a little run. Bernadin thought he must have seen a wild animal. A little farther on, the horse made another bolt, breaking into a gallop, and this time Bernadin had a struggle to hold him in. The horse fought, the heavy sleigh slewed in the wet snow, and presently a clearing appeared by the side of the road. And there sitting on his haunches among the stumps in the moonlight, was a great dog wolf with the moonlight in his eyes.

"The next afternoon a young man came to Bernadin to tell him that a wolf had been seen in the woods between the road and the St. Lawrence, and that the young men were going to hunt him the next day. Early the next morning before sunrise the hunters met together and with their dogs and guns began to search the woods leading to the shore. It is wilder country than it looks, a place all rocks and steep paths, rushing small streams and deep and sunken defiles. The young men hunted under the great morning star and saw nothing; they hunted under the morning sun and saw nothing. At noon they built a fire and talked for hours. Beginning the hunt again in the afternoon, they came at sundown to the heights of the ragged cliffs above the river. One of the young men suddenly cried out that he had come upon the tracks of the wolf. There they were, leading down a steep gully to a kind of rocky beach.

The dogs made a lot of noise, but were not eager to follow. As the young men came out of the forest and in sight of the river they saw the wolf. He had gone to the beach, run out on the great floor of ice above the shallows, and crossed to the open floes. It was getting dark, and the clouds were heavy and unbroken over the moon. From the beach, the young men could see the wolf on the ice, standing motionless on a great floe sailing with an outgoing tide toward the east and the sea. All fired at the floe, though it was far out of range and everything was melting away and becoming one with the dark. In the silence after the uneven crashing of the guns, all listened for a sound. For a little time all was still. Suddenly from far out among the floes all heard one wild and solitary cry which went on and on and on, never breaking till it died away above the ice. After that, all was still.

"No one ever again saw the young man with the grey eyes. He had left the house of his friends that same morning before sunrise, saying nothing to anyone. When they woke, he was gone. And that is the end of my grandfather's story."

THE FAREWELL OF CADIEU

In the days when the fierce and cruel Iroquois were lords of the forest, compelling the lesser tribes to tribute or driving them in panic before them east and west, in the days when the blackrobe priest of France dwelt in the Huron villages and took his sagamité of corn and moose meat from the common dish, in the days when the first young Frenchmen were forgetting

the faraway inheritance of the older earth and becoming fur traders and adventurers, in these times, and on
a spring morning, the coureur de bois, Pierre Cadieu,
and his Indian wife arrived at the portage of the seven
chutes by the rushing Ottawa. Their canoe with its
baled and corded furs stowed amidships was soon concealed in the bush at the beginning of the wild descent,
and man and wife made their way into a little clearing
marked by the charred wood of Indian fires. The day
was mild, and the small birds who winter in the south
were returning to the evergreen forest across the great
St. Lawrence and calling out to each other in the sunshine of spring, and at the beginning of the carry skeins
of paw marks had traced their delicate paths among the
rocks and clays. Never quite out of ear or mind, the
roar of the great river thundered beside the open path
of the carry, pouring and tumbling on across the smothered ledges and the furious and sunken cataracts.

The woodsman and his Indian wife had wintered
in the forest, moving their lodge about in the trees and
snow and hunting and trapping as they moved. Now
the snowshoe days were over, and as soon as the Indian
friends had arrived with whom they had made a rendezvous at the carry—Huron hunters each with his
winter spoil—all would go together down the river to
Montreal. After much tossing of the furs upon a counter and much opening out and displaying of the pelts,
the king's money would change hands, and glasses of
brandy seal the bargain. Good Christians, all would next
wander to the church, once more to thank Heaven for
their preservation.

The sun was still above the trees when those for

whom Cadieu had waited arrived at the carry. These were five young Hurons coming in a party of two canoes, each boat, like Cadieu's, well stowed with furs. A moon close to its first quarter stood above the clearing in the higher west, growing brighter with the closing of the day. A pot of deer meat was boiling away in the dark close under the trees.

Suddenly one of the young hunters made a quick and warning gesture:

"The Iroquois!"

A small war party of the enemy had crept up unseen and were lying in ambush across the carry. There was but one hope. If the raiders could be lured away from the path, the Indian wife and others of the party could hurry their canoes along the portage trail to the end of the white water, and take to the river and paddle for their lives. Difficult by daytime and strewn with destructive ledges, the passage below the rapids would be almost certain death by moonlight, yet it must be run. If the plan succeeded, those who had led off the Iroquois would rejoin the others farther down the river.

Taking one of the young Hurons with him, Cadieu melted into the darkness of the woods, leaving the others waiting in a tensity of silence on the dark side of the clearing. A shot rang out, and after an interval another at some distance from the stream. An ululating war cry, shrilled by some single Iroquois warrior, now rose from the woods, dying away in the moonlight, and then there was silence again till a scatter of distant shots was heard from the heavy growth away from the portage. One of the Hurons scouting ahead, the wife of

Cadieu and her companions now rushed two canoes and their furs down to the end of the portage. A thrust from the shore, and the wild water was about them on every side, shadows and shadowed waves and rocks all one in the moonlit miles of turbulence.

None heard a cry and the beginning of a death song, but the Huron companion of Cadieu had fallen, mericfully dying in a few minutes of his wound. Cadieu himself was badly wounded as well, his left shoulder being shattered to the bone. Hidden between two great pines, with the Iroquois moving in their Indian silence on his track, he stanched the wound as he could, and waited for the darkness which would follow the setting of the moon. When it came, he began to work his way out of the portage woods. He would never, now, rejoin his wife and his friends. If they had reached the rendezvous at all, they could not linger there, but must press on, and the Iroquois would be watching every mile of the bank. Some miles away there was high and rocky country with good concealments and ledges from which one could spy out over the forest. In the sharp cold of the morning, his shoulder, outwardly numbed, burned with an increasing inner pain. Remaining hidden all day, on the second night he reached the higher land, finding himself a crevice of refuge by a pool of snow water lying shallow and cold on a rocky shelf. He was dying. The great sun was rising in the sky, but his own day was darkening and coming to its end. Into that twilight would vanish all that had ever been, his young and faithful Indian wife, the presences of his companions bending to the paddle as the current grew strong, the forest and the winter and the snow, the frozen horizons of the great fresh-water seas under their somber weight of cloud, the feel of snow melting on the face, the smell of birch smoke rolling off above snow, and the sweet fragrance of fir balsam, the taste of deer meat and corn in a pot, and the sound of rivers heard in the spring throughout the wilderness, the unceasing roaring living in the milder air.

On sheets of birch, peeled from a near-by tree, with a twig for a pen, and his own blood for ink, he began to set down a song of farewell. Across the forest and the years, from a thousand campfires and Canadian hearths, the touching song has come down to us and the touching and simple melody.

"C'est donc ici que le mond' m'abandonne." Would that the "petits oiseaux" had been able to tell him that his wife and his Huron companions had arrived in safety at the Lac des Deux Montagnes! It was getting dark. When searchers from Montreal found him on his rock, he was dead, his arms crossed in piety upon his breast.

THE FIDDLER OF THE NORTHERN LIGHTS

There was once a family of habitants who were clearing land in the valley of the St. Maurice when that country was still the forest. The land of their choosing was not on the river, but above it in the woods, and they had sheltered their house and a first field behind a low ridge of upland on the north. A road led from their clearing down along a brook to the wild St. Maurice, passing the houses and cabins of a few neighbors who were likewise "making land." Beyond the ridge there was nothing of man, only the empty forest and the empty sky, and the night's fixity of the North Star.

Early one night in the autumn there came a knock at the door. A stranger whom no one had ever seen stood waiting in the dark. It was bitterly cold, but he wore neither greatcoat nor mantle, yet he carried under his arm a box wrapped in the pelt of a black bear. In aspect he was a man of strong middle age, made older by a crown of snow-white hair.

"But you must be cold," cried the kind mother.

"No," he replied, "I am not cold." And it was true. His hands were as warm as if he had just risen from before a comfortable fire. The family did not press him with questions, and he offered no explanation of how he had come to the house. It was taken for granted that he would spend the night.

As the evening lengthened, the visitor asked the family if they would care to hear a little music.

"Mais avec plaisir, monsieur!"

Before the eyes of mother and daughter, before the interested glance of the father and the two grown sons, the stranger unwrapped the bundle of bearskin and disclosed a black box. Within it was a fiddle black as a coal with an ivory bridge for the strings, and a black fiddle bow with hairs from the tail of a black horse. When the fiddle began to sing, the family knew that no one on all the wild St. Maurice had ever heard such playing. No music more beautiful could have been heard between the wild St. Maurice and the gates of Rome. The family sat enchanted. What a guest to walk in out of the woods! Would he stay with them awhile so that they might ask the neighbors in to hear his playing? They would give a veillée, and there would be songs and dancing.

Yes, he would be glad to stay a day or two and play for the veillée.

The next morning there was a little fall of snow, but on the day following it cleared as it can clear only in the north, and the neighbors were invited that evening to the house. News of the stranger had already reached the other farms so everybody who could manage it came through the forest to the party. Rocking chairs and stools were pushed aside, and an open space cleared in the rustic kitchen. The stranger did not at first play. It was the youngest son who played for the dancers on a fiddle of his own making.

When the stranger saw that the dancers were ready to be quiet awhile, and that the company were hoping he would now begin, he took his black fiddle from its black box and began to play. Beautiful as the music had been before, now it passed beyond and away from the earth under the fingers of the fiddler, leaving the wild St. Maurice and the woods to roam in the spaces of the sky. Each note sang pure and strong as a bow of light, and like light itself, changing, broke as it were into many colors. The guests of the veillée listened in a silence deep as the quiet of the forest, young and old halfway to another world.

A young man, hardly knowing what he was doing, or why, opened the door and looked out into the night. The sky was burning with the splendor of the northern lights. The mysterious low arc of pale phosphorescence which spans the north stood boldly across the pole, the

WATER FRONT, MONTREAL

dusk beneath it gathering into its solemnity all the lonely darkness of the woods. Out of this arch the vast rays and paths of the aurora were breaking in their pale and terrible fire, some ghostly as the arch itself, others touched with an icy green, the vast gleams shuddering and glowing, swaying and seeking, vanishing and reappearing among the dimmed stars of the halted constellations. As the young man watched the lights in their play, he became aware of a wonder beyond the world of man, of a thing so marvelous as to be scarce within belief. The great beams and paths of the aurora were keeping time in the heavens with the music of the fiddler! When the music changed its beat, slowing to a measure all solemnity and sadness, the fingers of light moved with the same great melancholy in the north; when the notes sang faster from the bow, the beams swept the heavens in their own high and radiant dance. The young man beckoned others to the door. Awestruck, the company watched the splendor and the mystery, crossing themselves and uttering each a prayer as the aurora followed the music over and across the pole.

"Speak!" they cried, falling back in terror from the fiddler. "Who are you, stranger? From what parish do you come? Are you at peace with God?"

The stranger laid down his bow, and rose to answer them.

"I am of the north," he said, his voice solemn, yet bold. "My parish is the snow. I have no longer a name. Beneath the lights I was born, beneath them I have lived, to be one with them I have sold my soul. The power I have is of Beelzebuth, Prince of the Power of the Air.

"Do not fear. Do not fall back to the wall. Do not tremble that I have shared your bread. See, the lights are fading from the sky. The dance is over, and I must be on my way."

With his black fiddle returned to its black box, and the box itself wrapped in its black bearskin, the stranger turned to the company in ceremony, and walked out into the night. All watched in awe as he stepped from the lighted kitchen out into the dusk of forest. Those nearest the door said later that he had not turned his steps toward the villages, but toward the north where no man was.

To this day when the beams of the aurora are sweeping in splendor over the wild St. Maurice, there are old folk who say, "They are dancing to the music of the fiddler of the northern lights."

Even as the lower Alps have their Wild Huntsman of the clouds, and the cities of Flanders the merry Tyl Eulenspiegel, so the shores of the St. Lawrence have their own legendary hero. He is a figure of the lumber camps and the lonelier villages, but he is not Paul Bunyan; his adventure is one of the mind rather than one of Gargantuan powers; in his bottes sauvages and with his ax over his shoulder he is "the spirit that denies" in the world of spruce and snow. He is "The Young Man who had been in the United States," the young, oversure skeptic who is certain that wonders do not happen. Alone in the camp, he refuses to share the traditional beliefs and superstitions, dismissing the tales of his companions and the cautions of his elders with the liberated assurance of a traveler who has learned better over the border. No, he replies, wonders do not happen. But they do. They happen to "The Young Man who had been in the United States" all through the forest and all up and down the river with convincing and usually fatal results. Sooner or later, this Excelsior of skepticism, banner and all, gets just what he deserves while the wind from the forest, the bitter "Nor'oua" of the snows, shrieking, proclaims the triumph of belief and mystery.

Your true folk hero lives more in speech than in books and both "The Young Man who had been in the United States" and the following tales here make, I think, their first appearance in print. Here are two favorite stories told of what happened to this unbeliever.

On a winter's morning a crew of woodsmen left their camp and trudged off towards a cutting in the spruce. As they walked on together into the forest, they saw ahead of them, staring down at them from the branch of a dead tree, a great white owl . . . l'hibou blanc.

"Well, that means no work today," said the foreman. "Come, let us go back."

"Go back? Why?" said one of the crew. He was a young man who had been in the United States. "Just because we have seen a white owl! That is foolishness."

"A white owl means misfortune before night," answered the foreman. "It is not foolishness, and we are not going to cut today." The other men nodded their heads. "Come, les gars."

"All right, go back if you want to," said the young man. "I shall go on alone." And with scarce a word to the others, he shouldered his ax and trudged on into the wood. His companions were troubled about him, but they knew that he did not believe or care.

Gathering together in the lengthening afternoon, the men who had not gone to the woods smoked their pipes in sociability about the stove, and waited for the return of the young man. It was time for him to be back in camp. The shadows were already growing hazy upon the snow, and the cold of coming night was strengthening in the air. In an hour it would be dark. But there came no squeak upon the snow, and no hand upon the door. The crew began to be troubled for the young man. He should have been home with the sun. Getting into their coats and winding their scarves about their necks, they decided to go in search of him at once.

In a little while they came to the place where the white owl had been seen, but the bird had gone. In the gathering shadow and cold they could see their own trails on the snow, the many tracks returning, and the trail of their companion going ahead alone. All hurried towards the part of the forest into which he had gone.

It was dusk when they reached the glade where he had been working. A huge tree had been chopped down and lay cradled on the snow, and beneath its branches and to one side, there was a glimpse of a coat and a mittened hand. Crushed by the fall of the tree, the snow in his eyes, lay the young man who had been in the United States.

He was dead.

In a lumber camp of the pays d'en haut, in the high country of the spruce forest, a crew of woodmen were telling stories and legends about the Devil and his tricks. Above the frozen sea of trees, the stars of winter burned in the fierce sky, but within the camp it was warm and good about the stove, the pipe smoke rising blue to the lamps hanging from the beams and wreathing up past the chimneys to the eaves. Each man had a story to tell of some adventure of the Devil on the river. On a lonely island he had plunged out of the forest, taller than any man could ever be and blacker than any coal, crying out against the church bells as he fled; here he had waited at a miser's door in the shape of something that was now a toad and now a stone. In spite of these stories there was a man of the crew who dared to say that he did not believe in any such tales! He was a young man who had been in the United States.

These words made everybody uncomfortable, and for a few minutes nobody moved or made a sound. Suddenly the camp door flung itself open wide into the night. As there was not a breath of wind stirring, all wondered what could have happened, and one man rose from his chair to close the door again. Scarcely had he taken a first step when a terrible apparition appeared at the door. It was a giant black dog with a coffin bound to its back. Falling back before him, the woodcutters shrank to the wall, and the dog entered the camp and lay down before the stove.

"He has come for one of us," said the foreman, his voice husky with fear.

"For one? What one? How shall we know?" said many voices.

"We must each of us in turn lie down in the coffin," said the foreman.

. So one by one, going properly by seniority and standing, the men of the crew climbed into the coffin and lay down. Whenever some lad of a pure life and spirit took his place, the dog stirred no more than a stone, but when some man whose soul was blackened by a sin extended himself, the dog struggled horribly as if to rise to his feet, snarling and grinding his teeth under the load. It was terrible to see, yet the dog never fully rose.

When the turn of the unbeliever came, he would not take his place or enter the coffin, but fought his way to the wall, whence he watched the others go one by one to the test. At last all but he had faced the coffin and the dog.

"Come," said the others, "you, too, must go. Yes! You must take your turn, for the Devil's dog is not to be denied." And closing in about him, they caught hold of him, and forced him over to the coffin, pressing down his legs, and straightening him out within.

The moment the young man was laid in the coffin, the black dog sprang to his feet, and lifting his head, uttered one terrible cry. He then crossed the room, his eyes burning like coals, and clearing the threshold, dashed away into the night, coffin and all.

More and more distant, farther and farther away

under the stars, the listeners at the door heard the diminishing yells of the young man who had been to the United States. He was never seen again, never, never again!

"Le Pulp"

I

IN THE last of twilight on the river with the great stream rushing past some country pierhead under the slopes of the Laurentians, the wanderer in the valley will often hear a sound coming with a broken monotony out of the cold and advancing night. It is the xylophone klunk of pulpwood being tossed from some truck over the side of a wharf into a pulpboat waiting below, billet striking billet with the same hollow and wooden sound till the last falls, and with a roar the truck vanishes, a momentary light, on the road into the mountains. In the water below, in the rising and chafing tide, the boat swims in its masthead radiance, figures working there with hooks and peavies, their abrupt shadows following like ghosts along the decks. Presently the lights go out, a domestic glow in a cabin window darkens, and the mountains, the river and the night gather all of man into their peace. At sunrise all is still. The boat has gone with the tide. Yet within a day or half a day, you shall hear the sound again, hollow, wooden and reiterated, and so goes the spruce forest to the mills.

Of the various craft using the lower river, the pulpboats are entirely the most familiar. From sunrise to the dusk they pass, their Diesels hammering the air as they follow some inshore swerving of the channel, both boat and sound presently to melt away together in these river immensities of blue. In design they remain the most seventeenth century of modern ships, being but so many small, old-fashioned luggers, rounded in the bow as a baroque shell, and hollow within as cradles,

the single mast serving as a derrick to which one may in an emergency bend an ancient sail. Aft rises a two-story deckhouse—more of a carpenter's structure than a sailor's—which serves as a bridge above and as cabin, galley and engine space below. Go aloft, and you will find the wheel, a thwartship bunk seemingly too small for any comfort, and a calendar and a crucifix on the wall.

Go below, and you will find bunks and a galley, a wood range with an old smoke-blackened crucifix hanging sorrowful above, the usual, the indispensable rocking chair, some two three old books long ago read to pieces, and the year's tide tables hanging well-thumbed upon the wall.

Almost invariably these are family ships. The owner-captain carries his household with him as he goes. Beyond the pleasant forest smell of the spruce load, beyond the line of diapers quiescent in the twilight and the shelter of harbor, a peaceable haze of wood smoke and cooking is sure to mingle at the open stern with a male reek of home-grown, habitant tobacco. In port or on the river, the woman of the house comes and goes out of her galley parlor, or knits in the rocker carried out on deck; dropping things only to hush the wail of a baby or attend to some other small child unsteadily wobbling about. Hard as the seasonal work may be, because all are French aboard, everything becomes in its way a social occasion, and in the very middle of the loading you will hear talk and gossip and discussion and, often enough, a few bars of a song.

I often wander down in the Laurentian twilight to some country wharf, and watch the loading of such a boat. The work is old-fashioned heavy labor, a thing of the old, direct, physical contact with life for which only the old and natural acceptance, the old arrogance of physical strength and the old good will, can prepare the muscles and the soul. Last night quite a large craft came alongside at sundown to wait for a load here and to spend the night. The baby linen had been taken in for there was something of a threat of rain, but a baby's chamber nested forgotten against the galley wall. The woman of the house remained invisible. Because of automobiles and the new roads, the wharves are now deserted of the little steamboats of the past, and "le pulpier" had the forsaken landing to itself. Two young men, seemingly kinsmen, had the craft in charge, and were smoking cigarettes while waiting for a truck. They were aware of me, and I made them a sign of the hand which was courteously returned. Short, chunky, and French, rivermen and boatmen from a town rather than country men gone sailoring, both were in a sense transatlantic brothers of those workmen one sees in Paris, elbowing room for themselves at a bar. I say in a sense only, for the Canadians were harder and more wiry, unbedeviled either one by nerves or "bistros." Two trucks arrived that night, one hours later than the other, and from my near-by house, I heard till I fell asleep, the familiar noise continuing. A little after midnight came a sudden and awakening roar of rain, and looking out, I saw that the wharf was all in darkness save for the navigation light winking on a shed.

In the morning, boat and boatmen were gone, having taken advantage of the clearing day and a rising tide. Bound for a paper town west of Quebec, the craft would spend the entire day upon the river. Somebody would bring out the rocking chair and contrive a nook for the cradle and the baby, and the mother who had remained unseen would look at Quebec on its rock, and watch the excursion steamers going to the Saguenay. Early in the northern dusk, foretold by a universal reek and stink of sulphur and wooden rottenness, the mills

and their stacks would appear beyond some huge void
and darkness of the river, the fabulous mountain pyramids of billets drenched in their eternal searchlight
glare, the conveyor dropping fresh sticks down upon
the cone, and the great mill windows green with the
abstract horror of electricity. But the next evening it
would be the mountains again, and the blue dusk-
shadow of the mountains, the clang of the Angelus in
the cold and dying light, and some deserted wharf for a
nights mooring. East and west along the river, the
bright pin points of the navigation buoys would trace
the channel with their measured wink and stare, and
when all was still some listener aboard might hear from
the greater silence ashore, a far sound of one of a thousand cataracts.

II

The farmers and the villagers of the St. Lawrence
are the builders of these ships, laying down their keels
by some convenient creek in the tidal meadows below
the cliffs. Plank by plank rising along the sides, they
take their wooden shape in the salt hay, the river glim-
mering beyond, the swallows soaring above, and the
sound of hammering drifting over to the road. All summer long the village here has been building such a boat,
the path to it from the road growing every day more
matted and muddy in the August haze. During the hay-
ing season I noticed that she stood deserted in her scaf-
folding, her builders having forsaken the calking mallet
for the scythe. Some family group of the village is behind the venture, but the entire community is imagina-

tively interested and has kept itself informed of the
work from day to day.

The great event in the life of such a craft is not its
launching but its formal blessing by the parish priest,
and I went yesterday to the ceremony. Standing new
and unpainted in the marsh, the hulk had turned into
a little ship, her deck hammered down, her last plank
shaped and fitted to her ribs. We have been having the
year's hot weather, and the prairie heat of the Mississippi west has been flowing down the valley like a second
giant stream; the familiar blue American haze has lain
like wood smoke on our landscape distances. It was
Sunday, and a fine afternoon. At two o'clock villagers
in their dark and hot-looking Sunday best—they do not
go in much here for summer clothing—began making
their way to the ship, and I could see others walking
about and talking on the deck. One by one reaching
the ship, each climbed aboard by a ladder propped
against the bow, and one by one were made welcome by
the owner-builder and his kin with that natural good
breeding and courtesy which is a heritage of French
Canada. It was hot, and there was no shade on the little
deck lifted into the air. There was nothing to do but
take it easy, talk and walk about, and watch the river
and the road for something to catch the eye. It was by
road that M. le Curé would arrive.

Measured time is a city invention, the deeper one
goes into the country the more it loses its urgent peev-
ishness, and we waited for some time on that rustic
deck. There were now some thirty or forty people gathered in the sun. Babies had been wisely left home, but a
small boy and a smaller girl walked in sociable propriety

with parents touchingly young. On the distant road two figures stepped from an automobile. The priest of the village and his curate were arriving. All hats were raised as they came climbing aboard in their long soutanes, and one could feel the general satisfaction and the personal liking in the gesture of respect.

M. le Curé had been for some years with his flock. He was a man of middle height, and somewhere in his younger middle years, and there was that in his frank and pleasant face which bespoke quiet authority and a wise and friendly spirit. After a short discussion at the bow with the owner and his kin, he put on a stole, and sprinkled us all with holy water. There was a general movement of the making of the sign of the cross. A quiet came down on us like the quiet which comes in church. The curé was about to speak.

"My children," said he, standing book in hand and a little to one side, "the life of man is like a voyage, it has its good weather and its bad; its hours of sorrow and storm, its quiet of harbor and its days of peace. Let us ever remember to seek strength from God, that we may endure the difficulties and temptations which lie upon the waters, and overcoming them, be worthy of the paradise of the blessed and the saints." From this simile, he went on to speak of the ship he had come to bless, asking for her God's blessing, that she might be strong on the wave, outlast the gale and storm, and prove a prospering venture for her people. From this prayer of his own in French, he turned with a pause and a gesture to his book, reading to us the ancient Catholic prayer for the blessing of a vessel, the phrase *ille nave*, coming now and then to my ears out of the sonorous measure of the classical syllables. Another turn about the deck with holy water, a litany with responses, and *Le Bon Canadien* was ready for the St. Lawrence and her task. M. le Curé took off his stole and closed his book; there was a little time of easy and friendly talk, and then home we went in groups across the marsh.

In a day or two the boat was gone, having been launched on a night tide. At some larger town a shipyard would presently fit her with a derrick rig and an engine, and the abrupt and northern autumn would probably find her on the river with her pulp billets stacked on deck, her new paint rubbed by the wharves, and a line of washing hung astern. Such vessels, they tell me here, are sometimes built on order, sometimes as a speculation; others are handled by the builders themselves and the wheel confided to some seagoing kinsman, le fils de l'Oncle Joseph, or le Cousin Pierre.

"Le pulp"—the word has become a specialized French-Canadian noun whose comic ugliness would kill a French academician—is with agriculture the commerce of the lower river. All the long, fierce winter in the back country of the spruce forest and the arctic wilderness of snow, the young men cut the trees, dropping the snow-covered, groaning evergreens down into the universal white. In summer the stripped and measured lengths will be standing in stacks by every farm, weathering there in the dust and rain of the wild roadside, a dense growth of bunchberry closing about the lowest tier. All day long the trucks will be laboring and lurching their unsteady way up the hills, only to disappear in a downward rush and a cloud of dust on the other side: at night oxcarts will be winding down a ravine to give a pulpboat a load at some ice-wrenched and homemade pier.

"Le pulp", it is a savage business, a commerce of pure destruction thoroughly bad in the long run for the psyche of any people. So far there seems little relation between the cutting and any rhythm of forest growth. Nature is there to be sacked and the fierce attack goes on. Time and the spirit of man, I think, have turned against this pattern of the world. Sooner or later, guided by its own intelligence or by bitter necessity, a civilization will again remember that visible nature is not the immediate spoil of an age or its generations, but the timeless inheritance of man, the ancient mystery to be forever shared with those who forever are to come.

CHAPTER NINE

Sunday on the River

I

A FEW weeks ago while wandering about on the south shore, I chanced to spend the weekend in a French-Canadian town of the agricultural kind, coming in the evening to a large old-fashioned dwelling serving as an inn. It stood a little distance back from the street and at the eastern end of town, a cottage-mansion painted white with a trim of royal blue; above the door a single electric light, burning in a frosted globe, opposed a bleak radiance to the deepening beauty of the night. Beyond it stood a gigantic church, and beyond the church the country and the fields. It was August but the air was already autumnal cold. Would there be enough bed clothes? I wondered. The French keep themselves warm with light coverlets which might be just so many antimacassars; I need more. A great *galerie* or raised piazza extended across the façade of the dwelling, and there I waited the answer to my ring. Presently appeared a woman of middle age, our two faces meeting in mutual inquiry under the impersonal downward glare. Dressed in something black, she had a knitted shawl upon her shoulders; I thought her face good-tempered and intelligent. Could I have a room, madam? Si, monsieur. Come in and I will show you. Il fait froid, n'est-ce pas?

It was a house, as I had suspected, of the Golden age, all old-fashioned paneling inside with heavy paneled doors, the whole interior painted a rather merciless enamel white and floored, corridor and room, with the hard modernity of linoleum. French Canada has a national passion for that convenient covering in its newest furniture-store designs: serviceable or not, it would be difficult to find anything with less sentiment. For some reason or other here the very great virtues of the people, the native good will and sociability together with the gift for family living have little reflection in the interiors and the domestic arts of life. Seen from the road and judged in terms of architectural line, house after house is rich in character and interest: few things in all the north have more charm than various old French farms in their provincial rusticity, but go within and you will find yourself in a newness curiously without past or mood. Only too often the best of it is a certain cleanliness without interest or warmth. One must remember, I suppose, that comfort and the grace of living with both beauty and ease are English gifts to civilization; it is from beneath chimney pots and the November fog that the chintz-covered and comfortable chair, the tea urn, and the open fire have gone forth into the world. On his return to England from Waterloo was not the great Duke of Wellington's first and initial order for "plenty of hot, buttered toast"? Not only has the French temper never achieved the secret of such living, but also has it never managed to learn it, and it is significant that the language has had to take over the English terms.

It is in the kitchen that the French-Canadian house

becomes alive, speaking here of farms and dwellings of the wider countryside. What is native and traditional, what is of the earth and the patient hand has here a kingdom of its own. Here in a shelter of old-fashioned wooden walls humanized by wood smoke and pipe

smoke, the family gathers at ease about the wood-burning range: here the ancestral crucifix hangs above the table and the bread. The more important school and church diplomas of Patrice, Marie, Jean, Wilfrid, Marcel and little Cécile are trophies of these walls; in a corner stand the books which will be read again on a winter's night; here the calendar, gift of the local garage, counts the holy days and the months and brightens the

wall with a saint's portrait in primary colors. Plenty of
strong, old-fashioned kettles and pans of iron stand by
the range, and I remember one friendly hearth where
a row of Montagnais birchbark containers, all over a
hundred years old and as black as the stove, still held the
staple supplies. Such memories of the Indian and his
arts were once far from rare in the older parishes. The
Algonquin has influenced the habitant farmers far more
than he has the Yankee yeoman across the great frontier,
and only a few days ago in the Laurentians, and in the
very sound of the village Angelus, I found an Indian
cup of birchbark by a spring.

It is from such a kitchen that the visitor, if he is
lucky, will have a partridge stewed with onions in the
habitant style—and a good recipe it is, and better than
serving a roast bird tough as a slice of leather. There is
no more excellent cooking of its kind than countryside
French-Canadian. French provincial in its tradition,
simple and good in its recipes and wisely skilled in its
simplicity, it lives wholesomely and well from its resources of farm and field. On the north shore, if you eat
with the family, you will not find white sugar in the
bowl but maple sugar scraped fine. A particular touch
of old France is the excellence of the omelets: you can
get a good omelet anywhere, not the whipped-up egg-
foam monstrosity, but the true French thing, the small
omelet of tradition beaten with a fork and fried in
country butter. Serve this with a wedge of honest,
home-baked bread, a pat of butter to one side, and a
bittock of homemade wild-strawberry jam, and one's
hunger and weariness make their own grateful prayer.

But I have long said that a good loaf of bread is in itself an offering and a prayer.

I was shown to a room on the northeast corner of the house. The west wall of the chamber which contained the door had kept its old and handsome paneling, but the other walls were papered in just such a brownish and grandiose miasm as one might have found in France itself. Somewhat to my surprise, the double bed, instead of being the usual affair of iron loops and fancies, was a mahogany piece of the Louis Philippe age, an imposing engine it would have taken an entire family to lift from its place. There was linoleum on the floor, and a devotional picture on the wall. From the geometric middle of the ceiling, from the very navel of the clean flatness overhead, an electric bulb of lowish power, suspended from a cord, brightened the chamber with a defiant if somewhat feeble modernity. Homes of the French countryside have no encouragement for reading in bed. The room was all of one piece; nothing could have been more proper, orderly, and clean, and I put down my knapsack with grateful relief. Later on, another guest arrived in the person of a salesman from Quebec smoking the inevitable strong cigar. I heard him talking with Madame, a parade of voices passed down the corridor, a handbag bumped my wall, and then Madame came quietly back and turned out both the hall light and the bulb above the door.

As I was not yet sleepy, and the hour was only a little after nine, a mood came over me to leave my four walls and rather cheerless glim and walk about on the *galerie* awhile. The outer night had grown very sharply cold. Townwards, the shops were still busy with Sat-

urday night, but between the inn and the lighted shops
two neighboring houses had already darkened their
windows and gone to bed. Across the street and over a
level emptiness of fields, the river had become one immensity with the dark. Standing in its open space
beyond, the titanic church lifted to the night its soaring
towers. Following these spires to the sky, one saw the
portent which dominated the dark of the world—a
great pathway of the northern lights arching the river
in a glowing transfiguration, all else in the heavens nocturnal and serene. Seemingly as motionless as the Milky
Way, the vast bridge towered over the mountains and
the huge impulse of the stream swept by its own waves
and agencies of power, now growing fainter but not
faint, now glowing again from shore to shore in some
cold and luminous surge.

When I went again indoors, returning to my room
along the lightless corridor, the quiet of the house was
responsive to a low murmur of prayer. In the kitchen
Madame and her servant were saying the evening rosary,
that chaplet of the Virgin which in so many French-
Canadian houses closes the ritual of the day. In a little
while I heard from my room someone locking the outer
door for the night, and after the passing of these steps
there came no other sound.

II

I woke to a first great din of bells. Masses begin
early in French Canada, and the Sunday bells announce
not only the first service but proclaim the mood of the
day. It is the festival of the people which they sound

from their granite towers, bell after bell swaying and thundering in the quieter Sunday air, parish echoing to parish on both shores of the river till some last spire to the east scatters its brazen outcry over the beginnings of the sea. There are no bells in North America like the bells of the St. Lawrence. They do not play tunes or chime, they are not rung in the English peal but are tumbled all together even as they are in Spain, tenor and bass and silvery treble clashing and clanging together in their wild and momentary harmonies. It is the festival of Heaven, it is the festival of the people and the race, and the village is getting into its best things while Wilfrid is harnessing the horse.

There are noble bells at Trois Rivières, and fine bells at Quebec, and a beautiful, mellow brotherhood in the church at Bagotville on the Saguenay. I am told that they are usually of French or Belgian origin, and have come to Canada from the ateliers of the old world.

It was a lovely morning, and the bells had their own awareness of the sky. In the serene, open light the St. Lawrence seemed a brighter blue that it ever seems to the north and below the mountains, and far away the hills themselves faced across into the sun. There seemed no one at home when I went prowling about for breakfast, and I imagined that Madame and her servant had gone to early mass. The house being so still, I returned indoors, and having found a plush and linoleum parlor, began to write a letter. On this I was well embarked when the door opened and Madame returned from mass amid a clash of bells for the next service. Bonjour, monsieur. Bonjour, madame. I have heard of faces shining—would one saw more of them!—and I

can use no other word for her countenance. Honest and
good in itself, there now beamed upon it a kind of good-
tempered humanity and Sunday satisfaction which was
not without an inner touch of gaiety. Churchgoing on
the river, I remembered, was both a religious and a social
festival, and once the mass had been heard and shared
in, and the congregation dismissed into the sunlight and
the genial day, there followed no Sabbatarian gloom but
a time of talk and greeting and exchange of news. It
was from this double satisfaction that Madame had returned to us, her religious duty done, her human sociability and curiosity refreshed and enlivened. As she
vanished into the kitchen, there to put on her apron,
poke up the stove and get breakfast, I could but reflect
on how much the expression on a countenance was
capable of changing over what life might physically
have done to us, the expression on a face being like
light on a landscape, capable of magically changing
mood and line.

So Sunday began, a French-Canadian Sunday on
the wide St. Lawrence. The morning, I remember, was
the church's and the curé's, the bells ringing, and everybody coming and going in their Sunday clothes. The
older women wore the respectable black of France, the
younger women what they could find at the nearest
large store of the day's American styles. The clothes of
the men too were the American ready-to-wear conven-
tions of the moment, but chosen out of the darker and
dingier shades, and not worn as by the rangier and more
tense American. It is a folk custom of this people for
the men to separate themselves out of the congregation
leaving a service, and wait about awhile on the steps of

the church: with such a scene begins *Maria Chapde-laine.* So it was on this pleasant morning, the male assemblage in its clean but completely cheerless propriety of dress remaining under the towers to bandy jokes and have talk and smoke a first knock-me-down pipe of home-grown tobacco. What a forest of matches such steps are on Monday morning! In a little leisurely while the farm carryalls and buggies began driving home, each vehicle freighted with population, the occupants positively terraced on the seats, and child after child after child fitted seriatim into each other's laps—the baby on top—like a nest of cups. It is part of the day's custom to use the best horse—and to give the habitant his due, his horse is a good beast and has a well-fed and comfortable air. Now and then it is an old car which careens by as full of people as a belfry is of starlings, and only too often being driven as dangerously and badly as a car can possibly be. The mechanical gift almost universal in America is not one of the inheritances of this race—when it exists, it is an individual affair—and driving and driving behavior on the French St. Lawrence are the least of my admirations.

In French Canada practically every family dwelling has a piazza running along its front—the *galerie*—and to the galerie as an institution belongs the sociable Sunday afternoon. Though houses in the smaller towns do not actually touch they are built rather near together, and a side of a street on Sunday afternoon may seem an almost continuous piazza. There is no shelter of any kind, and every thing is as public and open as a steamship's uncovered deck. Family by family, there is

all the town in its Sunday ease, some piazzas entertaining, some welcoming callers just arriving, others merely resting and taking it all in. The scene has its picturesqueness, and there is nothing else quite like it on the continent. The *galerie*, itself an institution, is the triumphal arch of still another very French-Canadian institution, the rocking chair, *la chaise berceuse*. From one end of the river to the other, a dwelling without a rocker is like an egg without a yolk. One finds hereditary rockers in the kitchen, a mail-order rocker in the parlor, rockers on all the family boats, and a possible rocker in the woodshed. Sunday afternoon is the festival of the chair. There is scarce a *galerie* on which somebody is not seated in a rocker, and scarce a rocker which is not being determinedly, decorously and soothingly put through its familiar paces.

The whole picture of such a Sunday afternoon is an illustration of the ability of the people of the river to manage a good and sociable time in a very simple way. I remember well one afternoon of early summer when all along the galeries of an old-fashioned country street people were eating and nibbling fresh stalks of rhubarb as if they were a sort of local lollipop.

Perhaps the most deeply rooted of all old-fashioned customs is the veillée, or neighborhood "sociable," of the winter nights. This is simply a kind of local party given by some family at its own house, friends and neighbors being invited in for a good time of everybody's making. The friend who can sing will have the floor for a selection of old national songs and a possible French translation of something American; "Home, Home on the Range" having many versions. The local dancer will dance his local variety of eighteenth century jig or even launch out into a tap dance of the great world (probably learned from "the young Man who had been to the United States"!), the local violinist will scrape, the accordionist "oblige" as we say beyond the frontier, and the vaudeville finished, everybody dances. They like waltzes. Then follow refreshments of a kind, and finally the party breaks up, driving off with a fine counterpoint of sleigh bells into the intense and almost arctic night.

CHAPTER TEN

A Pause by the Current

I

ALITTLE civilization, organized, compact and growing, has been created on the river. Within the fabric of a British dominion, it lives the life of a French and Catholic nation, fitting its medieval heritage both to the machine age and to British law. The adventure is unique in the world of modern politics. The fiber of its strength is its religious conservatism, a force very intimately a part of our human nature, and in this case doubly and triply strong because religion is here both patriotism and history as well as traditional belief. In its own world, the province has achieved its triumph. It has met and subdued the hostility of the eighteenth century, it has created out of its small resources an intellectual world and something of an industrial order, and it has kept its identity, its beliefs and its tongue. The smoke has continued to waver and blow off from the chimney top and the cradle within has continued to rock; the colony has lived and the people have come through.

What of the civilization which has been thus patiently made and what of its mind and arts? Self-contained, isolated still, and in parts remote, with what

167

powers does it face what is left of the nineteenth century process and the ruthless terror of the new? There
exists within it a far more vigorous intellectual life than
one might at first believe, a life largely and admittedly
clerical whose books resemble those one used to find in
the older and more Catholic towns of France. Those
who know that France—or any France—will be amazed
at how completely French in manner and technic is this
literature. These devotional treatises from Quebec and
Montreal, these local histories and essays from all up
and down the river might have come yesterday from
some Parisian seminary and some press with windows on
the Seine. It is the French mind through and through;
it is as if all the vicars on Long Island wrote the English and university prose of the prebendaries of West-
minster or the Dean of York. The conversation of the
men of distinction of this world is again French in its
liveliness, wit, and intellectual curiosity: it is good talk,
and talk is a shrewd measure. Of formal literature by
the laity there is little to be found, a few books of
poems, a novel or two and the yield of the year is done.
In this lay writing there is a sense of literary inexperi-
ence, but it is an adventure on its way, and it is deeply
and lovingly interested in the life of the river. The intellectual world which is not clerical lives most power-
fully, I think, in journalism, and here again is the same
Gallic flair and intellectual relationship. Montreal is its
stronghold, and the best literary criticism is French of
very genuine distinction. The eternal logic of the French
mind rules the sequences, the prose exhibits the same
ideal restraint and pitilessness of form; there is present
the same ability to argue with power, clarity and dis-

tinction in favor of what life ought to do but never does. (Perhaps we do not consider enough the power exercised by the genius of a language over a national soul.) The river has its painters of landscape; there are famous names. A notable gift is a real feeling for the great music of the golden age; even in a village you may hear it played with skill and particular understanding.

The greatest of all outlets is politics, and politics can be a passion. (One is often told that when its interests are not materially concerned, the church does not seek to influence political action, wishing the laity to have its own world. It is certain that an open and unjustified invasion by the clergy would be resented and fought.) While living on the river I was often amused by noting how the pitch of voices actually altered when politics were discussed, an unmistakable tension vibrating the raised voices and the arguments.

II

Of the politics of French Canada I know nothing but I doubt if any lack of knowledge will envenom my declining years. Of the industrialism—largely absentee in ownership—which has become a part of the river I had best again hold my peace. It is industrialism as it is everywhere, a belittler of man and a destroyer of his living relation to the earth, and the people have been handed over to it with little wisdom or mercy. In this connection, an honest observer must set down that the people of the river are extraordinarily careless of their physical past. Outside of the kitchen, few houses have

QUEBEC FROM POINT LEVIS

a thing in sight older than the crayon-portrait age, and that is antiquity. (What can have happened to the later eighteenth century and the early nineteenth as it lingered with us in the thousand cupboards and parlors of New England?) It is true that the province was not rich and that its people got on with very simple things —witness the birchbark containers—but why should there be practically nothing left? Enter the fine old Norman cottages built at a slanting tangent to the road, and apart from a few amusing old-fashioned stoves shaped like minor wardrobes, the material arts of life reflect only the mushroom nineteen hundreds and the boom years following the war. Worse yet, instead of going to one side, roadmakers massacre the old beauty of the province as they will, wiping out great trees and fine old villages as if they were so much dirt, and there seems no one, no voice public or private, to stay their Yahoo destruction of the national soul. There is one destruction which is of God, and that is the destruction inherent in the renewal of life; the dead leaf must wither and crumble in the cold, the flower give way to the relentless pressure of the seed below. Opposed to this is another destruction which is of the Devil, a destruction without necessity and without creative future, a destruction only conceivable in age of the emptiness of the human spirit, and working itself out in brutality and the ruin of the heritage of men. Of this the earth is full, the smoke of the torment ascending, and it will need all the trumpets of Revelation to restore to us the earth which men have loved.

III

Pulp mill and industrial city, village and field, gigantic church and towering seminary, all rest upon one central pillar, the habitant who holds and works this earth. In the French-Canadian soul a kind of nostalgic piety, a real Latin "pietàs" surrounds the timeless figure, and you have only to wander in the bookshops of Quebec or Montreal to see how great a proportion of the writing in the valley is but a poem in his praise. The man on the hillside, the woman at the window blurred with snow—the figures are a part of both literature and the day's reality. I have at times thought this habitant nostalgia, poignant and tender as it is, this rooted preoccupation, a possible danger to other elements of the civilization needing help and praise, but after all, it is instinct and the depths of feeling which are involved, and who is to question their rightness? Great writing has touched the figure once—in the pages of *Maria Chapdelaine*. Let those who read, however, remember that the book is not a picture of French-Canadian country life on the river but an account of a family living in a new settlement and on a wilderness frontier. Poor Madame Chapdelaine, who will ever forget her longing for the life of the veille paroisse and nothing in sight of her kitchen but the stumps and the bush?

Louis Hémon's book is now almost a generation old. How do things stand today? How have Chartres and the dynamo fared side by side? Friends of the river tell me that almost everywhere, and in particular near the cities, the habitant is becoming—forgive the word

—de-traditionalized, the young holding their beliefs, but the old poetry and the customs blurring. The overwhelming world is all about their ears even when they return from the birches and the spruce. Their own politicians have copied American social legislation which is alien in deeper spirit to their way of life, the impersonality and the daylong cackle of the radio are on tap in many a kitchen, and modernity with a finger in every pie—but desolate and frustrate within—will have the habitant at the dance. Modernity has its charms; it tugs in one direction and custom in another, and it is not easy for a human being thus to be disputed and to be himself a part of the dispute. Friends also tell me (in a kind of an aside) that the world of the factories and the towns is not his oyster, that he is not an individualist but a man of a social tradition, no natural mechanic like the American, and that with uprooting comes an unwholesome wrenching of the personality. He needs his earth under his feet, and his own village about him. Emigration is a different matter. There he leaves his nation behind, accepts the stranger's way of life, and brings up his children as part of a new existence.

It is the rooted habitant, the man of his own earth, I have come to know upon this river. Sometimes he is master or the elder son of some comfortable farm, sometimes the sturdy, good-tempered younger son, born to no inheritance, of a log cabin in the hills. As a young man he wears winter and summer a costume that is almost a uniform—high leather boots (bottes sauvages) with wool socks showing above, a pair of darkish woolen pants, a wool shirt and windbreaker jacket and an old felt hat. Thus clad he ploughs these hills, scatters the steaming dung, sows the fields from a wallet at his side, and works a long day uncomplaining in the sun and rain and the cloudy squalls of snow. When he is a farmer, he is a farmer to the bone, and not a Martian looking for a crop. On this side we use the earth as if it were an automobile; it is used but not loved; the habitant both uses and cherishes the land. His deepest impulse to beauty he shows in the making of his fields. All through this country there are fields and great fenced meadows which are as green and lovely as any on the earth. He buys frugally, why should one have to buy? The fields are good, the bread is good, and the sons and daughters are ready for the day and the task. I remember taking refuge from a storm at a rather poorish farm full of people, and being there made welcome with the most touching simplicity and kindness. The mother of the house was spinning and turned her wheel as she talked, and the domestic hum wound in and out of the vast enclosing roar of the huge Laurentian rain. There is still a great deal of spinning done at home, and the socks made from this living, unprocessed wool, are the most comfortable of all things to wear. I buy them whenever I can.

There is one particular thing which should be said about the true habitant—the real 'Baptiste' of the old St. Lawrence—he may be very poor, he may have lived a hard and even a gaunt existence, but he is never vulgar. He has kept his birthright of human dignity. Bred to endurance, notably patient, touchingly content with little, sociable by nature and with this sociability reinforced by the communal quality of his religion and his life, honest, devout, and humanly "of good will"—there he is, and may Heaven prosper him and his furrow.

He has his problems—they are not easy of solution, and the victorious cradle, in one of its aspects, is the most difficult of all.

CHAPTER ELEVEN

Episode on the Côte Nord

I

THE scrub forest of the Côte Nord is known as "the bush". It is desolate country, a foretaste of Labrador in its rocks and loneliness. Save for a few settlements forty and fifty miles apart, there are few signs of human life. For hours the only human thing in sight is the telegraph line of the coast, striding pole after pole eastward through the solitude to the lighthouses beyond and the decrepit pulp wharves still standing at the mouths of the larger streams. All else is rock, the tongued splashing and roaring of waves, and the green-blue, flat and empty sky. I once chanced to notice on that coast—as I followed it in a boat—a tiny cove or sort of haphazard pocket in the reefs, and two or three houses isolate in the scrub. "Who lives there?" "Colonists." A few days later going up a wilderness river from an Indian village, we turned a bank that was but a great fan-shaped smear of sand. A wretched house of logs stood on its top amid a forlorn wreckage of stumps, and a huge dog coming to the edge of the smear barked savagely at us as we passed in our canoe. "Are Indians living there?" "No. Colonists. They came last year."

The famous cradle by the kitchen range has filled, emptied, and been promptly filled again. What is to be done with its living crops, with this ladder of sons in their bottes sauvages, and these little daughters who are learning to join in the family rosary? By a kind of primogeniture sanctioned by custom though unrecognized by law, the eldest son in French Canada gets the farm, and should they stay with him under the paternal roof, younger brothers must work for him and under him as family pensioners. The oldest son, l'ainé, is a person of importance everywhere. Sometimes no such arrangement is even possible; there is no room, and as soon as the new master marries, the relentless cradle will begin rocking again. The sisters may be expected to marry in the village and usually do. (Families who are comfortably off frequently have a daughter in one of the orders of the church. It is always a distinction to have a member of the family in the religious life.) But among the less fortunate, the poor young men must be off, the old felt hat passing out of view down the road through the spruce. Indeed they do not have to wait for a brother's overlordship to urge them on, they must leave their fathers and mothers, their village sweethearts and their community and be gone to earn their bread. The surplus young families too must go somewhere. But where? The country is far to the north, and the usable agricultural land in the older province has been extended as far as it is worth while to go. Emigration to America has been halted by American law and the condition of industry. The great Canadian cities take what they need from their own urban supplies of labor. The result is that the "colonization" movement, and the appearance of "le colon" as a figure of the times.

It is an official movement carried on by the government of the province and assisted by the church. The prospective "colon" enters his name, the government checks his case, and sooner or later if there is available land, he is sent out to it and helped to start. The young surplus families have the first opportunities; indeed the scheme is primarily a family settlement affair. During the Abitibi boom it was not unusual to see a group of young unmarried men and young fathers with their families meeting at the railway station to go to the north frontier. Each group was in the careful charge of some young and friendly priest, and it was all a touching thing to see. For some time the promised land was the Abitibi region which I have mentioned; in other words, the still unoccupied forest country lying well north of the St. Lawrence and the Ottawa and south of the forlorn shallows of James Bay. In latitude the region is only a little north of the territory so successfully opened about the Lac St. Jean, but returning colonists have told me that it is much more liable to summer frosts. Unlike the older pioneering towards better and better land, this modern movement is a spreading out towards worser and worser land and towards possible despair. Nevertheless, Abitibi is well established; it is no thriving golden vale, but people have managed to dig in.

Sometimes families are put wherever officialdom can find a nook or cranny, and pretty much left to shift for themselves. In the wilder regions of the river to the east, one comes upon various hungry and next-to-last-ditch adventures which are not pleasant to contemplate. (I have heard from French Canadians the bitterest of all criticism.) The church, of course, stands by, and its young men go anywhere and do their duty by the exiles. I have nothing but admiration for their courage and devotion. They take their place in the bush with their exiles and pioneers, camping out with their parishioners in the long, fierce winter; they follow the frozen rivers as did the missionaries of the past; they keep hope alive. One young priest told me of leading a band of colons into the north and into country so wild that they had to take to canoes. "How patient and good they were," he said, "and how they sang."

II

Last autumn I had my own encounter with this world in search of both a place to live and a place in life. At Matane on the south shore I had gone aboard the Clarke boat which crosses the St. Lawrence to the tiny settlements of the Côte Nord. It was but the nineteenth of September but the day was forlornly cold and greyish with a threat of snow. There was no warmth in the light anywhere, even when the cloud above thinned in its squally billowings of mist. The journey was to take part of the same day, the night and part of the day following, and I was glad to be taken promptly to a warm and comfortable room. I have forgotten the name of the vessel; suffice it to say that she was but a large motor cruiser painted white, and both shipshape and well-handled. Having had my share of the sea, I like to talk to French-Canadian seamen. The old Norman gift for seafaring has endured upon the river, and it is pleasant to find it living and at its task, with its sons wearing their gold stripes and anchors and giving orders on their ships. Indeed let me pay a compliment and say that the professional sailoring of the French St. Lawrence is far better than that of contemporary France. The people of the river have a better discipline and a far wiser understanding of discipline both officer and man; they are probably better trained, they are more on their toes, and they know how to give a ship its pride. It would seem as if the great British tradition of seamanship and the bold seafaring of Saint-Malo had united, much to the honor of the Dominion and the river.

There were but half a dozen cabins and only about as many cabin passengers, yet the boat was full. On the forward deck, in the cheerless wind and cold light of the ever-threatening day, some forty or fifty young woodcutters were being taken to the wilderness camps of the Côte Nord. Not a man among them, I thought, could be much over twenty, and some were but great boys grown to men. It was the world of the young who had to go. There they stood below, wandering the forward deck as soldiers do on a troopship, all of them in their working farmer clothes, their great boots, wools, and windjackets, each man with a packsack and his own personal ax. One gayer figure, a Norman blond who seemed to know his way about, had on a plaid windbreaker of the showy mail-order kind, and this enlivening garment served as a contrast to the country wools and elbow patches. Among themselves they talked in groups, visited and smoked. Some were dark, some blue-eyed; there were a few Scot-looking redheads, and a pair of brothers unmistakably and strongly French and Indian. There was no air whatever of sadness in the gathering, the good-byes had been said at the farms, and now there was work to do, and one's bread to gain. Now they would cut pulp all winter long in the arctic bush. I shall remember all my life those good, patient faces and those packs with the ax handles showing.

The young purser, a most pleasant intelligent lad, stopped a moment beside me at the rail, and we stared meditatively together down at the gathering. "Where

do they come from?" "They are mostly men of the south shore, farmer's sons from the poorer families. An agent, a 'jobeur', signs them on and after they have been given a medical exam, they are sent out into the woods. Some are making their first trip. All of them have papers . . . that's the red slip they've been looking at and folding away. The company agent has been here all morning. In good French, they are 'bûcherons'—wood-cutters, but the slang for them is gazasses (one of the thousand transformations of garçon?). We carry a lot of them. These here will be landed by groups. Some are sent ahead into the bush to prepare the camps for those who will follow."

By night fall we had crossed the river to the Côte Nord and were following the coast to the east. Hollow and pitch-dark, the night itself enclosed us, dripping with gentle and incessant rain. Somewhere to port lay the uninhabited wilderness, black as the universal dark and without the smallest glimmer of a light. At two in the morning we came into a bay, and feeling the engines slowing, I put on a coat and went on deck. The rain had grown a little heavier and there was a rising wind. We were in dark waters and somewhere off a pier showing one red electric light. Suddenly, with a stage-like alteration of the scene, the box-searchlight on the foremast went on, drenching the foredeck with its radiance, and revealing something of the nearer shore. It was a settlement of three houses, mere shacks in the woods. Close by the pier a huge pulp chute and tower, some relic of the boom, stood in melancholy and portentous ruin, vast as a Roman siege work deserted in the woods. On the foredeck, else empty, and in the haid modern glare and the stripes of rain, stood five of the woodsmen ready to go ashore. A little like a group gathered on a monument, they stood together, scarce moving at all, and none saying a word. Each man had his pack on his shoulder, the canvas spotting now with rain. A light presently shone feebly in some house or cabin ashore, and in a little while a boat rowed by one man came from the wharf out into the mainmast glare. Into this the woodsmen lowered themselves one by one overside. Somebody said something, someone replied, and then all was quiet again, and the boat plashed towards the shore. Turning and churning, our ship swung her bow to the sea, the light on the foremast abandoning the landward scene and leaving it to the immense recapture of the dark. During the night we touched at other settlements, and by morning the whole company had gone—packs and pipes, axes and tobacco, agents' papers and little treasured medals all moved up into the bush.

3
Quebec to the Sea

THE continent has broken apart. North and eastward lies an immense and widening rift into which the river has found its way, disputing it with the sea. To one side, far mountains descend in a sidelong wall to the stream, their crests notching an emptiness of sky, to the other, a fair twelve miles across, stands a confronting and lower rim of blue. Day after day this is a blue country, river and far coasts becoming all one panorama of a blue which is part of the huge and vaporous air. The blue of the St. Lawrence is not a blue of the sea or the sky, it is a blue of earth, a terrestrial mystery one in being with these huge shores and the great earth stream, a blue of the lower atmosphere floating over the dark green of North America. So vast a manifestation of nature has a strangeness of beauty together with that impressiveness inherent in aspects of earth on so great a scale, but one must not look for warmth. Changing in terms of light, paling or darkening with day and hour, it is fundamentally one mood of color, one dusk of blue gathering a whole continental region into its composure and austerity.

Some twenty miles to the east of Quebec rock, looming above the northern shore, the Laurentians begin with a bold headland rooted in the stream. It is Champlain's Cap Tourmente, the dark and outpost tower of the mountains, little changed in aspect, one imagines, since the day when a fury of water at its base gave it an enduring name some three hundred years ago. Enclosed between its sudden lift and the high rock of the city, narrowed between the St. Lawrence and the more rugged wilderness country which has fallen back to the north, lies Quebec plain, an open agricultural country spilling down to the river like the fan of a glacier reaching the sea. It is uplifted on ancient rocks which are grey to black in color, and over their edge, between a greenery of trees, the Montmorency pours its sunlit cataract. Villages sprawling into suburbs occupy the shore, each with its great church of stone and coldly-silvered spire.

Leaving Quebec reach, the ship channel swerves to the south to follow the pleasant rural shores of the Isle of Orleans.

So Quebec falls behind, a narrows of rushing water and a rock, an old city and a new, a place of ships and modernity, a place of cannon and walls and a noble sound of bells, the north and the wilderness fixed at its gates, and the clouds beyond it tinted pale to the far shores of Hudson's Bay.

It is again the morning. The beginning day is pleasant with sunshine and midsummer warmth, the river is busy, and the enormous scale of the broken continent to the east invests the entire scene with a quality of drama. Every great landscape imposes something of its own measure of earthly time, and there is something here of that debatable mystery.

Field beside striped field, farmhouse and barn, church spire and tiny summer villa, the pleasant shore and broad upland top of the Isle of Orleans sail along beside the ship. To the south another upland stands with mainland fields and farms above, and a fine precipitous shore of cliffs and trees. One by one, incoming ships pass flying astern the colors of many nations; a churning sound, a smell of oil and iron, an exchange of casual stares, and they are gone towards the narrows and Montreal or the wharves of Quebec. Island and island-passage ending, the width of the river opens ahead, a sidereal stream now, almost a part of space and the sky.

The Laurentian mass has risen above the river to the north. It is as a coastal wall that the higher country begins at Tourmente, shoulder after shoulder of grey archaic rock fronting the new immensity of the river, with occasional small glens or forested gullies hid between. Save for a next-to-invisible railroad managed at the base, there are few signs of human occupation, and one goes as along a local solitude. The channel now holding a northern course, the south shore dims to a blueness withdrawn into a serenity of dream. Far across, islands lie atop the stream like the crests of all-but-submerged mountains, their blue-black lengths melting into one appearance with the blue of the southern coast.

A first break in the northern wall, a first river mouth at Baie St. Paul, and the traveler has a glimpse of the farming country inland, and of the mountain rims and valley contours of so huge an earth. Still following close below the Laurentian scarp, the ship channel now enters the narrow passage between the mainland and the eight-mile length of the pleasant Isle aux Coudres. The stream races, a darkness descends from the towering shore; one might be at the beginning of a fjord. Mountain shapes and Laurentian domes, trees dark and austere, have replaced the wall, their forest colors and earth blues lifted between the passage and an increasingly colder sky.

A second opening at Murray Bay, ninety miles from Quebec, discovers the hidden country of the ranges to the north. Like blue mountains out of a fairy tale they rise, outposts of the wilderness rolling mile upon empty mile to the end of earth and of all human things.

Beyond the bay, its beautiful vesture of cleared and planted fields overlaid with cold Laurentian air, lies the great ridge of the open coast which the farmer has made his own. Like a long mountain it stands compact of other mountains, the colored crops climbing its pale sides, one road of villages leading eastward along it in a succession of metallic spires. A curtain of spruce hides the half slope, half precipice of the actual shore, covering with a green which seems here more sylvan the monstrous confusion of grey and tumbled rock confronting the wide St. Lawrence stream. As one passes, the same ridge takes on to the east a growing look of the frontier, clearings, cuttings, and the forest mingling together on the slopes above in traditional hostility. Seen from a ship, the coast on the level of the eye seems to present a grim and unbroken front of rock. Concealed by the perspective, however, are wild crannies and inlets and amphitheater coves: plunging rivers descend to them, their green silence is broken only by the sound of cataracts and the confused wash of waves in a confusion of rock, and sea birds swim all untroubled in their peace.

Now fourteen, now eighteen, now a long twenty miles across, the river is widening in its giant path. Distant but substantial still, at once a part of illusion and the solid reality of earth, the south coast remains in sight, continuing to the east its blue and impressive parallel. An island lies midstream, flat as a shadow on the river and overgrown from end to end with trees— the uninhabited Isle aux Lièvres. Mountain shapes and the forest now take over the north, a lighthouse marking all that seems left of man. Presently from the shore comes a new gleam of light on cliffs of sand, and a vast discoloration overside. The traveler has reached Tadoussac, the mouth of the Saguenay.

The coastal lift of the Laurentians is dying out of the scene. A new country lies ahead, falling off to the ever-widening east, a coast of bold terraces and rock occasionally widened below with tidal flats and salt-hay fields. It is a frontier country of frontier fishermen, farmers and cutters of pulp, a thread of human life along one adventuring road.

Fifty miles beyond Tadoussac and a fair hundred

and fifty beyond Quebec, the road comes to its present end at the Portneuf River. Sand bars, miles long and lying parallel to the coast, lead the tributary forth into the greater stream, and half conceal a valley which might have emerged but yesterday from under the glaciers and their sands. The caribou drift here betimes, moving down through the ragged firs to the river plain with its bog vegetation and winding miles of scrub. The coast beyond (La Côte Nord) is the coast of wilderness America. An inconceivable shore of the chaos and savagery of rock topped with a stunted savagery of trees, it remains the country of the trapper and the Indian.

The south coast has vanished out of one's consciousness. Far away, certain of its hills rise in the east like blue and solitary isles, very beautiful in their shapes of earth. All else is the St. Lawrence, and the long wilderness to the north with its brow of green and its surges breaking below. Miles to the east and north will lie the Point des Monts and the white tower of the light, the sudden turn of the coast to the north'ard, and the vast opening of the waters of the gulf. White whales appear, swimming well in toward shore. A change has come over the look of the river. It has put off its earthly coldness of white and the cold of steel, its strange colorlessness as of level miles of rain. Having broken free of earth, it has come to an end as a presence of earth. This is the sea and the north and the cold, final blue of the sea.

CHAPTER TWELVE

St. Lawrence Sky

I

Over this landscape of mountains and climbing roads, over this great river with its shores of farming lands and gathered villages stands a sky which, more than any other sky I have chanced to live beneath, is blended into a noble unity with the earth below. It is not in its essence a sky of clouds at all or even a sky of cloud, but a sky of primordial vapor of cloud, an elemental substance and presence of the mist dwelling in the northern air and in these winds, and seemingly arriving out of nowhere and into nowhere vanishing. It achieves a kind of form, becoming one dense and universal body during the night; it returns to formlessness with the warmth of the morning sun, dissolving to a texture in the air. Now, and only too often, a melancholy pall of rain and fog filling the whole sodden world with the deep-toned solitary cries and answering choruses of the bewildered and invisible ships, now a wild aerial wrack floating like rolling smoke across the silver-whitened sun, it can make of any one day a wayward series and variety of days. Dramatic, unpredictable, and very great in its own aspects of beauty, the sky is here an integral part of human life and the day's experience, a mystery touching every thing that lives with its fantasies of change.

It is the vapor mass of the lower St. Lawrence to which one looks, that continent of water and air born of the entrance of the colder sea into the channels of the earth, a mystery of currents and tides and of the warming and cooling of these northern surfaces and the outlying ocean streams. Once the fierce openness of winter is at an end, and the cold and laggard spring comes over the snow with mud and rain and the sound of forest cataracts, the mystery gathers, standing dark in the wilderness sky or drifting down upon the river in its first advancing tongues. So protean is its nature, however, that it seldom occasions a true summer of grey skies. What it brings into being, especially during the early summer, is a sky all vapor and light and fantasy overhead and an earth immersed in transparencies of vapor and cloudy light as in a sea. A paler sun shines, the torn and transparent wraiths drift over the vast contours of the earth, arriving from the north and east and from over the empty mountains, hour by hour rolling off like smoke from some monstrous fire of the gods. Passing over at a height of some seven or eight hundred feet, and keeping well above the landscape in its drift, it is cloud wrack for all nearness, having neither the look nor the character of fog. As it flows, a new experience and pleasure await the eye. So vague, so unsubstantial are the beautiful and fragmentary shapes that cloud shadows do not follow them below, resting upon the solider earth with the antique majesty of the air. It is a new drama, a drama of light, which now appears in the wide scene. Out of some wild tatter of the veil, swimming as with its own motion forth from a vaporous obscuration, the sun of noon and afternoon is forever palely adventuring, taking to itself some sudden aspect of the countryside. Now it is a farmhouse with its woods and fields which stands enclosed in the pool of burning yet dewy light, now an island in the river, now perhaps a field of charlock in flower far up among the hills. Near and far, village and field, all is substantial: there is no sense of blur, but the air and the mood of nature are touched with water and the spirit, with romantic solemnity and the northern dream.

Beautiful as they are, the colors of this sky are cold. There is but little red in it at any season or hour and the touches of rose which come at sundown have a way of appearing in the east. Fog or gathered cloud, the sky remains a tableau of the tones and austerities of grey intermingled with a northern blue and a rather cold and silvered white. There is an evening gold on the mountains to the west, but it vanishes swiftly and without warmth into the dark.

Inland winds from the west and southwest blowing hot and dry are hostile to this sea of wrack, but winds from the ocean favor it, and strengthening it with ocean fog, roll the mingling masses before them up the river. I once saw such an oncoming, the very sky itself all storm and darkness to the east, advancing up the river like a wall. Pressing forward in a towering solemnity of huge and opaque densities, streaming vapors and wild aerial wrack, on it came, advancing between the darkening mountains westward into the open sunshine of the other half of day. Eastward, in and below the mass, the country streamed with rain. In spite of it, work continued in the fields and on the roads, the huddled groups, the solitary figures laboring on in the wet, for the habitant makes but little of rain and faces all but the very sluicegates of heaven with his patience and endurance. Coming out of the deeper woods, I saw in a first field to the right, a young man ploughing with a black bull and a black horse harnessed side by side; back and forth through mud they ploughed, opening their rainy land under the deepening and the thinning showers. And because it was baking day, the fires in the outside ovens were burning fiercely in their caves, their smoke and flame licking out of the doors into the streaming of the rain. Coming out of the mountains to the lower road, I left for a moment the storm behind me, and from somewhere above the Isle of Orleans beheld Quebec in the distance still enclosed in a pleasant summer light of the later afternoon. The overtaking storm again drew near; it began to sprinkle and grow dark, a churchly and familiar sound of bells suddenly gave a voice to the land, and from the next height of the road, above a river silvering and misting to a ghost, there was no more a distance or a city.

II

It was from the slope of a Laurentian hill, by a thicket of spruce which sheltered me a little from the north, that I used to watch on the warmer summer days, the gathering and massing of the vapor into clouds which are like no other clouds in all the wide Americas. About a mile or so below, at the foot of the cleared lands and beyond the road and a bordering of spruce, lay the river, widening to an ocean presence beyond the dark serrations of the trees; to the left and right were mountain headlands, and inland and unseen the wilderness Laurentians lifted to the empty air their distances of blue. Such sounds as came to me upon my hill were human and country noises, the French voices of reapers in a field or a shout to a horse in the universal language

men employ. Below, people came and went about their houses and barns, farm carts rolled off on adventures, and on the river passing ships moved with their modern air of business, smudging their smoke trails for a long moment on immensity. Across this scene and its humanity rolled the clouds, the midsummer monsters and titans which have perhaps no similars on earth, clouds which, becoming a part of one's awareness, cannot but touch the thought and mood with which one muses on the life astir below.

It was the height of summer and there was a new sky. (The earlier waywardness of mood, however, was near, being but a moment round the corner.) With the lengthening of the season had come hot and even burning days, and with them the cloud wrack had risen above the heated earth, the earth veil of moisture below never quite dissolving. In the higher and colder air, the great vapor mass was now breaking and gathering and shaping into separate and titanic mountains. Still so full of fantasy was the vapor overhead, and so mutable the great midsummer shapes, that the generalities of cloud nomenclature would have been hard put to it for exact and defining terms. Cumuli-like in their definition and in their woolpack convolutions and towers; unlike cumuli, they had no flattened and shadowed base on which to sail. Separate alps, sailing continents of vapor, the light fell on their billowing and rolling undersurfaces as well as on their peaks. Over the mountains and my slope they came, less clouds of earth than clouds of some planet on an ampler scale; cloud titans unimaginable floating suspended in mythological heavens, and passing in mythological splendor across the fields of ripening oats and the silvered belfries on the dark Laurentian capes. In one such great and solitary cloud I saw once at twilight the lightning playing with a white and silvery flame, burning in the aerial valleys and striking snakewise behind the giant promontories.

Arriving at the river, these masses drifted out a little over it, making their boldest ventures forth from the mouths of tributary streams. Once above the river they encountered there, it was clear to see, the colder temperatures and separate winds of the great stream for they towered up from the coasts as against an invisible obstacle, rearing up as it were affronted, their heads in the northern blue of heaven and their feet upon the darker blue of earth. Now and then their reflections like rippling pillars spanned the vast width of the stream. With these mountains tugging at the coasts, and the long reach of paler sky above the river given over to mare's-tails and long and windy wisps, the St. Lawrence has a cloud pattern very much its own which it repeats the summer through.

Though all nature be motion in its secret essence, to the human mind much of it seems fixed in an eternity of stone. Only a demiurge, some spirit or immortal creature could be conscious of the unrest whose long instant is to us stability, could be aware of the continents rising and sinking, of the seas gaining and the seas withdrawing, of the mountains taking shape and wearing away in the murmur of the rain. We are conscious of change, the field succeeds to the forest and the snow melts from the slope, but change even in our world may be either too swift or too slow to be seen in its working. Clouds are a part of the motion of nature which is visible and familiar in the earth we know; they are one with the unquiet of the wave and the beauty and the activity of fire. Changing from moment to moment, children of the air and the uncertain winds, ever the same yet never the same, they hold the eye with their mutability and the imagination with their permanence. For all their transformations, no other great manifestation of nature remains, perhaps, so constant and unchanged. The rocks break, the mountainside falls in the winter night, the coasts retreat, but the clouds gather and pass as at the beginning of all things, drifting across the sky, and trailing their momentary dusks of shadow over the mystery and splendor of the earth.

CHAPTER THIRTEEN

Wild Life of the Stream

I

A GREAT landscape is a kind of stage which like a theater must have its actors and its play: without its drama of living things, without the comings and goings of life, it is but a scene whose silence and quiet will come in their time to weigh upon the heart. It is not enough that the clouds pass over or the wind comes with violence and rain, that the sun leap from the bright sea or sink behind the darkening passes of the mountains, the drama of visible life, the poignancy and beauty of the world of living things must be a part of both the scene and ourselves if we are to enter into that mystery of exultation which is a part of the being of the world. A mountainside of barrens and nakedness of stone is one thing under an emptiness of empty sky, it is another when a hawk and its shadow slant across its vacant austerities: even the sky itself is touched with a new power. In a certain great perspective which is both mystical and of knowledge, life and the earth are one. There is not a region beneath the moon which life in some form or aspect is not seeking to invade or has already made its own. It beats upon us from out of the seas; it is part of our every step; it dwells in the vast oceans of the air. Confronting the valley of the shadow

of death stands the mountain of the sun of life at an immortal noon, a height shining above the earth and the
spirit of man, and whose mighty affirmation we oppose
with death and with death darken and chill only to
bring nearer our feet the neighboring shadow and the
cold.

The mightiest of all pageants of nature and the
earth was once our own—the wilderness miracle of
ancient North America. Varied and abundant as was
the natural life of other continents, the American vastness, sharing or even surpassing the prodigality, brought
to its great scenes a quality of drama like nothing else
to be found in all the world. The wild pigeons in migration, drawing near at sundown with a tumult of cries
and wings, and like rain from a cloud suddenly filling
with their mystery of life all the visible air; the great
buffalo herds following the green tidal rim of spring
northward along a thousand miles of grass—there was
nothing like this under any other sky. It was no small
part of the spectacle that migration routes were large
and uncomplicated and that the great simplicities of the
landscape, the long coasts and the immense mountains,
the grasslands and the mighty, southward-flowing
streams, spanned summer and winter in their course.
In so vast a sweep of climate and space how dramatic
must have been the great autumnal migrations, particularly those of the sea and coastal birds which followed
the long beaches and marshlands of the east! Flocks
were large, and every bay and inlet scurried by the
bright autumnal wind, every creek winding through
the fox-colored marshes of October would have been
full of their stir and talk, their wheelings into the wind,

and their sudden and warning cries. Like some great coil of ocean moved the immense river of wings, the birds flying out of the eye of ocean to the solitary beach and the peace of coming night.

Such was the wilderness, more nonhuman than inhuman, on which the American fur trade descended in its intrepid and destructive activity. The killing was no small matter for the fur bearers were annually slaughtered, specie by specie, in their tens and twenty thousands. It was the nineteenth century, however, which ended the pageant almost as if it had a purpose to empty the forests and the air. Armed as no era has ever been in history, provided man, woman and child with all kinds of precise and newly invented weapons, it descended on the animal world to make a devil's emptiness on earth. That a relation of beauty and interest existed between man and the creature, and that another relation, poignant and mysterious, existed between the human spirit and the animal spirit never seems to have entered its mind or heart. In the picturesque and rowdy forties, the killing was simply a battlefield of carnage of everything that moved or flew. At the end of the happy period, North America was no more. Like a great church whose windows have been stoned out and whose beauty sacked, it had become something else and something less. What we have today we owe to a mere handful of men and women, and may theirs be the woods of Paradise and their own reflected image of the earth of their desire!

No, we did not lose all. If you would still see a spectacle worthy of the Indian past, you have but to go to Quebec when the snow geese come annually to the

cap Tourmente in the largest single flock of migratory
birds known on the continent of North America.

II

Every year they come, arriving out of Greenland
and the polar north, great birds white as snow. September sees them descend and first hears their returning
cries in the autumnal dusk, a few arriving ahead of the
migration; then come larger companies; and last of all,
pouring in over the Laurentians, the great snowstorm
of the flock. The bird is the Greater snow goose (*Chen
hyperboreus nivalis*), a species breeding in the arctic
and wintering in the great open sounds and bays beyond
the Chesapeake. Measurements indicate that it is something the size of the Canada goose, but to the eye it is
a smaller bird. Take one from a gunner's hand (there
is a short open season) and you will see that the pri-
maries, whitish-grey at the base, are black at the ends,
a coloration which blends in many wings to a delicate
silvering. Forgetting smallest variations, all else is white,
and it is a certain duckyard whiteness which meets the
eye whether the bird is on the ground or in the air. A
gannetlike effect of wings tipped with black—though
pictorially right—is not really what one sees.

This year there are seventeen or eighteen thousand
birds feeding below Tourmente in one giant gathering,
and perhaps a thousand or so more scattered about the
neighboring islands and the nearer marshes of the river.
They will pass the autumn here, the white flock spread
for miles beneath the bright color of the Laurentian

woods; the wardens will see them on the marshes swept by the first grey squalls of snow.

It is pleasant country at the Cap Tourmente. For three hundred years the little region has been a fief of the church, miles of the north shore having been given to the clergy by Louis the Great, and even today there is something of the ancien regime in the rusticity. Quebecward, Ste. Anne de Beaupré has hidden itself behind a turn of the coast, and might even be the pious and simple village it was half a century ago, and the coastal road to Murray Bay has climbed the hillside and disappeared above. Below, away from traffic, are smaller houses and the one great farmstead of the Université Laval, all in a landscape of country trees and fields. Thus domestically rooted, the towering cliffs of Tourmente enclose the "petit pays," the silver glisten of a cascade threading a bright way over its lower steeps. One does not at first see the marshes or the river below. In such a place, particularly in the quiet field by the cascade where sheep munch and browse, the autumn is as much Rousseau and solitude as North America.

III

I began to see geese in the air as I approached the buildings of the household farm. Small gaggles and groups of the birds were crossing from the still hidden marshes to the orchardlike country just below the promontory. As one flock of ten or a dozen passed along the face of the cliff, I had the curious illusion of seeing their shadows following them along the rock, but lo! these shadows were not shadows at all, but an equal

flock of crows flying lower than the geese and nearer to
the cliff. Not till I had turned the corner of the shed
did I come in view, and all at once, of the marshes and
the flock. Then suddenly, there they were, miles of
snow geese, snow geese by the ten thousand feeding on
the meadows in a population as dense as a thriving
gooseyard—white birds as far as eye could see. The
incredible vista had something to it of the prodigious
and overwhelming together with something the air of
a farmyard of the gods. The nearer thousands of the
flock were in the very next field, the birds sitting farthest inland being scarce a hundred feet away.

Then came the sudden and completely unexpected.
From some gunner's shanty or blind beyond the farm
came a shotgun fusillade. With the first shell, and with
a simultaneous feathered roar, up went the thousands
into the morning air. Above us and about us the
October day, the cold winterish sky, and the very enclosure of space turned into wings, into a kind of
angelic storm whose long moment of being had no true
measure in the world of time. So vast was this myriad
arch and encirclement of wildly beating wings, so loud
the rushing thunder of its being overhead, that I had
in the instancy but little thought of the great birds of
whose lives the prodigy was made; the storm itself was
the core of life, overwhelming and confusing the sense.
Then, suddenly, it broke, the dome of wings and the
moment shattering, and the storm dissolved itself in a
higher sky into wheeling clouds of birds, into swift
hurryings full of purpose and alarm, and into faraway
and solitary escapes. Presently, like the air clearing of
a snow squall, space cleared of the universal splendor

of so many wings and the marshes covered again, gooseyard and miracle all in one. I heard no more shots, and
presently a church bell rang in the distance and brought
in a midday peace.

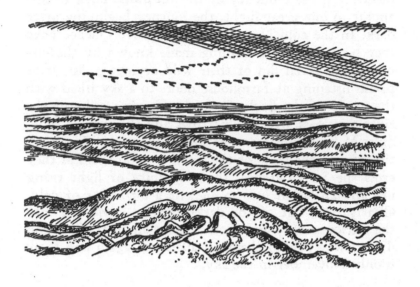

IV

The snow geese make two appearances on the river.
They come in the spring, arriving in early April from
the south, and remain by the Cap Tourmente till about
the tenth of May. With the first warmish days they
grow restless, and presently they are in the air, speeding
north over the forest to the farther barrens of the
north. The autumnal visit begins about mid-September
and lasts till sometime in November, much depending
on the weather. Below Tourmente the birds feed on the

thickened root of a familiar reed which is there locally abundant (*Scirpus americanus*) and appear to break camp only after cold weather has surfaced the marshes with ice and frozen-in the roots. Arriving by detachments, it is the tendency of the autumnal flock to disappear in one great flight, the journey beginning after dark. In the cold November night above Quebec have they been seen, their coming made known by the immense and aerial din of their wild crying, parish after parish listening at farmhouse doors to a sky filled with the music of the flock. Over the freezing miles of the river they pass, over the narrows and the ancient rock, miles of birds flying as a nation in the night. There are times when the glow of the town is upon them as they cross the St. Lawrence, the modernity of light rising like an exhalation into so ancient a bitterness of cold. Clearly seen, out of the darkness they come and into the darkness they go, their huge clamor trailing and dying away behind them till all is still again and there is only November in the sky.

v

It is when the tide is low, and the sea waters have fallen and withdrawn, that the St. Lawrence as a river reveals itself in its own incomparable power. Here at Les Eboulements on the north, a little beyond the beach, the tidal flats are covering over this morning in the coldish light of the warm day, each boulder with its shadowed side towards the noble contours of the land. So seemingly of the ocean is the region and the shore that I could easily imagine myself on some arm of the sea, and it is with a daily surprise that I watch the village cattle coming to drink from the tidal flood as at a pond. When these stones have covered and uncovered again, and afternoon has paled into the cold and tranquil sundown of this shore, there will be another awareness in the valley. It will be the presence of the great river itself, rushing seaward in the narrowed and deeper channel between the mountains and the mass of the Isle aux Coudres, the great St. Lawrence pouring like a level cataract, like a force of the planet itself, eastward into the dark. Past the piers it goes, living, elemental and troubled in its deep and glassy streaming with whirls and intricacies of force, a presence of beauty and terror scarce uttering a whisper in the night.

This is the great current of the deep north channel which bearing mountainwards beyond the Isle of Orleans, flows past the capes of the Laurentians to its daily mingling and huge conflict with the sea. Beneath these cirrus wisps and mare's tails of the over-river sky the vast struggle of which the outflow is a part sways daily to and fro, both eternal and new with every tide. The forces of sun and moon, the influence of shore-line geography and the slopes of the channel beds, the subtler interplay of specific gravities, these are but a part of the powers of nature engaged in so giant an encounter and so vast a scene. Certain definite patterns, however, exist in the unending war. The influence of the tide—as force—comes up as far as the Lac St. Pierre, the tidal momentum backing up the fresh volume in its unceasing outward rush. Quebec reach is fresh, and the harvesting of winter ice is still a part of its January calendar. A little downriver from the Isle of Orleans (the limit swaying with the direction of the tide) begins the body of water which is mingled of salt and fresh, the intermediate kingdom whose local salinity is a matter of any moment's elemental chance, and through whose depths currents seen and unseen pass in opposite directions, fresh and strongly brackish flowing contrariwise yet side by side. The eastern limits of this mingled volume must of necessity be vague, but there are certain agreed-upon frontiers. At St. Simeon on the north, a hundred and fifty miles below Quebec, the water begins to take on pelagic character, but the true pelagic salinity comes only beyond the Saguenay. Still another important landmark is the "Traverse St. Roch." Mariners never fail to speak of this narrow and shallow channel which cannot be passed at low water by oceangoing vessels, and call it, for their part, the true dividing line between salt and salt-and-fresh.

All this estuarine water is cold, some levels of it being just above freezing, and there exists within it a vast couch of arctic water suspended between two layers of a higher temperature.

So spacious a field of life, with both a giant order and equally giant struggles and confusions within the order, is sure to provide the naturalist with adventures. At Les Eboulements, as I have said, it was no novelty to see cattle drinking at the great north current, and glimpse beyond them and over their heads porpoises coming up the stream. Sometimes scarce a stone's throw may divide the natural kingdoms. On the north bank of the river, a little below Cap Tourmente and barely forty miles below Quebec, a tongue of a salt-water

current comes locally inshore, the ledges which divide
it from a fresh current being covered with marine algae
to one side and a fresh-water flora to the other. Pelagic
fish often follow such a saline path, but in general the
ocean species remain where they feel biologically comfortable. Such a pelagic fish as the mackerel remains in
the gulf and the ocean water; on the other hand, the
herring may come as far as Murray Bay. Moreover, the
river has its own "runs" of fish which enter the stream
and divide their myriads among the giant tributaries.
The salmon is one of these. Now following these species,
now simply exploring ahead, the giant sea mammals
enter the river, visiting on occasion all three life-areas.
A sixty-foot whale was recently reported aground near
Trois Rivières, and there is an eighteenth century account—given for what it is worth—of a large whale
having ventured as far as Montreal—the fabulous king
of ocean in the heart of the continent.

VI

Three creatures have a particular connection with
the river, being both a part of its natural life and the
human adventure. The first is the eel, for the St. Lawrence can at any time provide the world's heaviest catch
of these swarming and somewhat goblin creatures.
Greedy, averse to no food living or dead, and fantasti-
cally prolific even for the sea, the eel is to be found
everywhere in the St. Lawrence. The astronomical myriads people the river, ascending all the tributaries and
making their way into every lake and pool. Only Niagara halts their movement to the west. In the silences and

depths of the great north current the creature advances into the dark with its rippling undulations—so unserpentlike in their living shudder of force—but an observer is little aware, however, of its presence in the estuary or even of its role in commerce, for the region is vast and the inexhaustible millions give scarce an outer sign. The eel of the St. Lawrence is *Anguilla rostrata:* a species whose limits of distribution sweep from Greenland to Brazil. No other species is present in the estuary.

September and October are the great months of the eel fishery. It is then that the females who have gone on to the fresh water return in their millions down the streams, their long bodies flowing eastward with the rushing currents and the fierce, withdrawing tides. (Joining with the males at the estuary, the swarms then plunge together into the abysses of the sea.) As the creatures turn down the rivers to the meeting, the weirs and traps await their passage. The heart of these devices is a great cage of wood and wire well ballasted with stones and placed in the shallows at low tide, stout outlying wings of brush and small-mesh wire netting making a kind of welcoming V leading to the cage. Sometimes such weirs form a zigzag line and use a number of smaller boxes; other weirs are even more primitive, but are so laid down that escape is difficult. The creatures once trapped, it is the custom to bale them out at low tide and empty them living into a greater tank moored in deeper water.

Certain villages of the north shore are famous for their catch. They stand at the foot of the high Laurentian wall, hidden from all the world above by the overhang of cliffs and trees, fishing hamlets built unevenly along one street and darkened early with a shadow of afternoon. Creeping out into the sun, tidal meadows and gravelly flats there flank the eternal outward freshness of the great north current, and daily cover over with the widening invasion of the sea. It is across these submerged levels that the eels move, imprisoning themselves in the weirs and fences stalking out into the shallows from the shore. Though quite at ease by day, the eel is by nature a nocturnal creature; the night is its hour. Moreover, it prefers bad weather to good, and the catch is heaviest when storm and grey water lash the weir. Fair or foul, however, night after night they pass, entering the traps by some immemorial coil of the great stream, and filling the cold enclosures with their baffled, myriad seeking. The surface breaks, heads lift to some clear night of the autumnal moon and plunging leave arrows and ripples behind in the enclosed water, the long bodies peering from their nonhuman world into our world of night and air, thrusting out between life and death: the terrible, the heavy mass of dark and winding flesh increasing with every pulsation of the stream.

Once a part of international commerce, the catch was sold in both the old world and the new. Now the venture waits on time, carrying on as local industry.

VII

It is to the south shore that one must go to see the other fish which is so much a part of the adventure of the river. Less dramatic than the superb coast to which it looks and more peaceful and sunlit of northern afternoons, the south shore in its wider and more brackish shallows sustains a sea and river life with a character all its own. It is on this coast of sealike sands and marshes that one first begins to feel, I think, the ocean's nearness and increasing power. Fishing villages, moreover,

heighten the impression, the picturesque communities following one another down the coast, steeple by steeple, and cove by cove.

As you follow this route, you will presently see signs posted at the corners of farm roads leading river-wards—*Éturgeon* . . . Sturgeon for sale. Mile after mile they challenge the walker and the motorist, the white paint daubed crudely on a fresh board and the whole nailed any which way to a post.

If the word "ganoid" (the scholar's adjective for those ancients among fish which are many of them armored) haunted the somewhat fastidious imagination of Henry Adams, one has but to look at a sturgeon of the St. Lawrence to know why. No animal of terra firma, no monster out of Africa or Asia, carries such a suggestion of the world's prehuman aeons as this creature of the eternally nonhuman sea. The oldest and the first of bony fishes to appear in geologic time were such as these, armored and fantastic in the Paleozoic seas and streams. Descendant, representative and survivor of this archaic line, wearing armor still, having retained it across a million upon a million years, the sturgeon is less a proper contemporary than a part of the mood of nature which created the dinosaurs. The specimens one has the chance to study here are often quite large fish. Their color is nearly always a deep or somewhat muddy green—the belly being white—and in size they can be anything from six to ten feet long. It is not this impressive size, however, but an extraordinary quality of design which takes the imagination prisoner. The head is simply a steel shipbuilder's neat design of armor plates and sutures, and from this strange beginning a primordial row of great bony shields or bucklers—which look like fantastic barnacles and are like barnacles applied—armors the entire length of the midback. Two additional rows of smaller bucklers protect each flank, one placed well up the side, the other well down and not far above the curve of the belly line. The tail is of the shark type, the upper lobe being extended in a bold scythelike curve far beyond the lower. Such is the fish, half mythological monster, half contemporary, which returns with the early summer to the river.

VIII

The maple sugar has been gathered and the ice has gone, the last floe melting from its crevice in the marsh; the trees are in leaf and the rhubarb in its pride. The St. Lawrence has come to an end of its little season of ocean-blue, and the great vapors of the summer and the north are forming over the polar currents and the immeasurable wilderness. On the St. Lawrence, the sturgeon gear has been overhauled, the special traps and weirs rooted in the shallows, the strong poles pounded deep, and the boats launched which have lain so long against the barn under a cover of boards and snow. Presently a small item in the Quebec paper carries the news that sturgeon have been seen in the gulf. The fish are drawing near, entering the fresher estuary on their way to spawn in even fresher streams. Having toothless mouths, they must suck up their food from the mud, and hence follow the tidal shallows to the south. (Halfway across the earth, in the same first warmth, related monsters are entering the great rivers of the Russian plain.) As they come, the gravid females both outmeasure and outweigh their males. Nosing fresh-waterwards, a monster suddenly finds it can go no farther; indeed, it can scarce go anywhere. The first sturgeon of the year has been taken in the weir.

It is a capture, and a fine, encouraging prize. Fish have their own archaic dignity, and the imprisoned monster is gliding through its enclosed world with a kind of curious, uneasy solemnity, the scythe-lobe of its tail cutting the water like a living paper knife as it swims in perplexity just below the surface. With a first touch of a pole or an oar comes an instantaneous and unexpected lunge of violence, a movement made with all the body and the body's will. "Leaping sturgeons and dancing girls are hard to hold" goes an old proverb of the North Sea.

Either such a fish will be killed, cut up and sold at once—usually the fate of firstcomers—or placed in some secondary enclosure and kept alive till market day. The spawning run will peter out, the returning fish avoid the trap, but a well-stocked sturgeon pen can be drawn upon all summer long. Cuts of sturgeon are sold cheap at Quebec; it is the fish of the poor. Farm wagons driving into market on Friday mornings are very likely to have a great midsection of the fish stowed behind with the eggs, the chickens, and the milk.

The south shore is not without its cliffs, and now and then a sturgeon pen will be contrived in a gully of the rock which overhangs the river, the entrance being closed across by a rustic dam of planks and stones. The higher tides wash in, and a fresh-water rill may enter from above. It is in such enclosures that the great creatures wait, newcomers arriving with a prod and a splash, old-comers vanishing "of a Thursday." All fish pools are much one and the same, and these are but pools of giants, giants slow of motion and vaguely dark and dark-green, lost somewhere on the great river between Paleozoic and the table.

IX

It is always a pleasant thing when some great aspect of nature is associated with a tutelary animal; in such an association lives on the golden age. The river has such a deity. The tutelary spirit of the river, the fine creature who has made so huge a stream emotionally his own, is the white whale of the St. Lawrence, the giant white porpoise of the arctic and subarctic seas. What dweller by the river, watching either from a ship's deck or the height of some great cape can ever forget that bone-white turning in the blue world of the stream? Like a wheel turning in the water, the white appears, turns, and sinks in the vast plain of ripples and coiling eddies spread below. In my experience I have never seen the whale by itself and alone. The sight of a first is soon followed by the discovery of a second; presently some five or six or a company will be found wheeling and plunging by, coming like gods with the tide and like gods playing in the waves as if it were still the morning of the world.

It is in the seaward reaches of the gulf that one comes upon them in their greatest numbers. A few years ago on a bright morning of the cool, north-country summer, I remember watching from a vessel a company of a hundred or more playing in the broad passage of the Mingan channel, the level, empty wilderness and its flat sky behind them to the north, and all the water for miles gay with plunging white backs and a giant mood of ocean sociability. The creature is born mottled, a pale bone-white and something like khaki parti-coloring the hide, but this patterning is soon put aside in favor of the solid, the glistening, all-over white it wears in the St. Lawrence. When seen close by, it can be noted that the creature has no dorsal fin, nothing indeed but a great rounded back whose curving line it carries on ahead with its gamboling plunge. Adult specimens seem to be about twelve feet long. In the lower river, the Isle aux Coudres is usually considered to mark their western frontier, and so it may as a generality, but I have often seen small exploring companies miles nearer the Cap Tourmente. Small fish are a favorite food, and the whales follow the smelt coming up to spawn and the summer-arriving sand lance in its oceanic myriads.

The whale has long been hunted, and is hunted still. It was from these schools that the Indians of Tadoussac obtained the oil they once bartered. The Basques of the sixteenth century knew well the white plunge, hunting the creatures from their stations on the river: relics of their tryworks and furnaces are to be seen to this day. All through the succeeding centuries and sporadically on into the twentieth the old-fashioned primitive hunt and killing continued in the outlying eastern fishing villages, even as it does in these very times at places on the Côte Nord and French-speaking Labrador. The oil has its uses. It has a particular place, they say, in the specialized tempering of steel intended for watch springs and the innards of precision instruments. Given a further laboratory refining, it then serves to lubricate such devices.

The white whale, however, is no creature of industry, and please God may never be: he has a better and nobler role. What he brings to the great river, to these level miles of blue in their blue mystery of darkened air, is the gift of the presence of life: with that white turning these waters stir and live. The stream has its own mystery of life, it is all a tissue and a rivalry of life below, but we are little aware of that full press and swarming. That kingdom is not ours to share. Tumbling and diving in and out of that huge unseen, rolling up his white body to this human sun, it is the whale who makes these waves a part of the true image of the world.

I had once a memorable glimpse upon the river of that image as it sometimes reveals itself to the human spirit, all but beauty and wonder put aside. I was in a small boat, a kind of fisherman's launch, chugging eastward to the Indian settlements a long hundred miles beyond the Saguenay. We stood inshore to make the journey, the last farms and villages falling astern as we ploughed ahead, the empty wilderness succeeding, sunlit nearby and ominous beyond with dark gatherings of cloud. Fir trees, short and twisted and drawn up thick on a gigantically broken and rocky shore, passed us by for miles, the seas booming and leaping in this wild confusion, and breaking with a shatter of water and light on ledges scattered ahead. Early in the afternoon, the sunlight took on a cloudy glow, and in a few swift minutes there was a sudden pandemonium of furious and blinding rain. Then followed the veiled sun and the rain together, and presently the sun stood free in a great window of the storm.

There was vapor below—such vapor as follows rain at sea—and vapor sailing overhead; the sun again appeared, and all about us the St. Lawrence came into the restored light rain-lashed with trailing spume and foam. A mystery of color began to glow about us, touching the near land and the foam-running waves; we were in the magical world of the rainbow's end. Staring out into the colored sea, we presently found ourselves a part of a divine fantasy, inhabitants of the fabulous isle of Ariel and Prospero. Into that color which was air and light came the white whale. Passing close by, a school tumbled and plunged in its huge gaiety, the glistening white bodies glowing with the beautiful, the enchanted light, and wheeling over the delicate glowing on the foam. They passed and were gone, and the rainbow was in a little while as though it had never been, but the sun lingered, the storm piling up dark on the edge of the world like the tempest of Ariel's contriving—all else the St. Lawrence, the wilderness and the rock and a heavier sound of waves from the ancient chaos of the shore.

CHAPTER FOURTEEN

Small Birds to the North

I

To THE north of the great current and the tides, in that region of the Laurentian wall which borders the river from Murray Bay to Tadoussac, a kind of secret country lies between the farming uplands and the stream. It is the brim of the great Laurentian chasm, the region where the terraces and slopes above plunge in a forest chaos of rock, in a greenery of wild and picturesque descents, down to the remote and solitary shore. Sometimes old wood roads manage an almost headlong course to a retired cove but such byways are for the most part overgrown and have become tangles of wild grass and upstart trees. It is a country to know on foot for there are everywhere old and mysterious paths going about their ways with an almost Red Indian naturalness and secrecy. The plunge is deep, and the glens tumble four and five hundred feet to the hidden tides. Some aspects are of a real wilderness savagery. Others romantic and sylvan—it is here that the hardwoods flourish, the oaks and maples sharing with the spruce the shelter from the north—and there is always a haunting sound of brooks, a fountain splashing of cascades falling over succeeding shelves of rock down to the final levels of the beach. In this country of the

St. Lawrence to the north, these solitudes and glens enclose the kingdom of the smaller birds.

Who writes of birds must begin at once with saying whence he writes and I am setting down these lines in the pleasant village of Cap à l'Aigle, just to the east of Murray Bay. The village stands on a plateau above the glens, its cleared lands sweeping up behind it to a ridge against the sky beyond whose spruce is nothing— only the north. East and west along the river civilization is still one parish wide. Save for the dividing gash of the Saguenay with its power lines and isolated villages, all the back country is but the forest rolling in the cold wind over the mountains to the fog of Hudson's Bay. Of the birds who live on this frontier of cleared land and the forest and of the farming country birds below, I shall write on another page. Too little known to students of bird life, the St. Lawrence has its own particular miracle of birds, a drama vast in scale yet secret in quality and closely related to the country of the glens. It is the northward passing of the river by the migrant warblers who nest on this shore and in the northern and far northern forests of the Hudsonian zone. Considered as a family of birds, the wood warblers are distinctively American; they breed, most of them, in the coniferous forest, and all must cross the river to reach their other country towards the pole.

II

As the warblers move north, swept up together in successive waves of the migrational unrest, and forming, as it were, one dispersed army with its vanguard,

its center, and its stragglers, species and individuals fall
away by every mile. The Maryland yellowthroat will
find the blue Cape Cod pond he so often comes to
choose, the myrtle warbler his Connecticut glen, and
the magnolia his lakeside farm in Maine. Meanwhile the
invisible vanguard presses on, seeking the far north as
faithfully as the compass needle. The species who are
creatures of the evergreens, follow, I think, the evergreen forests of the east. Maine falls behind, and the
skies above the mountains, and now is the St. Lawrence
seen, and the other sky beyond, and the other and colder
light which is the north.

The flights begin with the end of May, and continue till about the tenth of June, the birds arriving
on these coasts when the new leaves are small. It is
through an awakening world that the warblers pass,
arriving every day of good weather from across the
miles of river. June has come; in the high country there
is still ice under trees growing densely together, but in
the farming land below the maple syrup stands in its
noble miscellany of bottles, and the dauntless rhubarb
of every French-Canadian kitchen garden has been
carefully enriched and hoed. Summer is near and the
plough is busy, but the Laurentian sun has still something of the quality of spring. Now is the time to visit
the lower woods. Not a trace of ice remains on the cold
tranquillity of the St. Lawrence. The spring wind is
light and coolly-warm, and in the cove opened among
the rocks the tiny, flattened waves make scarce a sound.
Only the deep-pitched and watery roar of a small cataract tells of the snow that once has been. Now, if you
are patient and fortune is with you—for nature is in

no showman's mood—you will see your birds. It may be
a sound that you will hear first, some pretty note of
summer practiced ahead of time in the solitude of the
glens, it may be something seen—a fidgetiness and a
poise of inquiry on a twig suddenly made to sway
above a stream. For miles along the coast, the whole
glen country is delicately alive with its facets of living
color, seen, lost and seen again in a sunlight and shade
delicately tinged with green. The birds are resting in
the wood, and will presently be off towards the mountains and the north. Tomorrow you may have neither
the smallest sound nor sign. The birds are crossing, I
imagine, almost everywhere, some individuals and species preferring an island stepping stone; others taking
boldly to the wider air. Some have come early, others
will be late, some will nest in these very woods, others
will be off at the unknown moment towards the Hudsonian immensities.

It is possible that here at Cap à l'Aigle local mi-
grants follow northwards the beautiful valley of the
Murray, that valley whose distant mountains are as
blue as those in some nostalgic fairy tale. I offer no
dogmatic list of the warblers who cross the St. Lawrence at this spot: lists are often a kind of folly. Be
prepared for the Canada, the Black-and-White, the
Cape May, the Myrtle, the Magnolia, the Black-throated
Green, the Yellow, the Yellow Palm, and the Northern yellowthroat, this last an interesting subspecies of
the more familiar Maryland. There are, of course, a
number of others: such a migration is always a living
cloud-drift of the customary, the possible, and the entirely inexplicable. Last summer, a hundred miles far-

ther to the east and near the mouth of a tributary stream, I chanced to see the Tennessee but I have never seen him here. Wilson's, too, is a bird reported from shores nearer the Gulf. Whatever the year may bring, the interest and beauty of the glens remain. The region

has its nesting birds as well as its passers-by. All through the earlier and warmer summers and all a pleasant day long—especially in the later afternoons—the glens can be full of a music you must go quietly down to hear. It is no choir of birds, no music box in the trees, but a music lovely, fugitive and capricious, an earth melodiousness of small and poignant phrases beginning in silence and in this silence ending. The small singer may be near, perhaps in the very arch of leaves above the path; he may be far away and higher up the hill, the song falling through this secrecy of space down to the opening and greater light beside the shore. Sometimes as I walk it is the song of the northern water thrush I hear, or the brisk, independent assertion of the yellow warbler, and often, very often, the "Trees, Trees, murmuring Trees" of the black-throated green.

It is not, however, the drowsy phrase of the black-throated green that I shall call to mind when I remember the glens of the St. Lawrence. The song I shall recall when I am far from the river is the song of the white-throated sparrow, that rustic arrangement in bird music of an opening call followed by three identical notes trilled as by a boy who can whistle with both a natural skill and a good ear. It is a pretty phrase, a kind of folk song of the woods. Indeed, it is because of its simplicity that it has been so loved, for though many things are admired, it is the simple thing which is loved of many. To us in New England the singer is the "Peabody bird" saying "Old Sam Peabody, Peabody, Peabody," but on the St. Lawrence he says "Beautiful Canada, Canada, Canada," or in French "Je t'ai vu Frédéric, Frédéric, Frédéric"—his English, to my mind, being better than his French. The white-throat is one of the good creatures who sing at night, and because of this the French of Canada call him le rossignol, the nightingale.

There are few adventures more characteristically and poignantly of this country than a walk in the glens when night is at hand and the bird is singing. There was a cataract in the glen country to which I used to walk in the early evening, coming to it across the fields and through the woods, discovering at last a huge and sudden amphitheater ringed with trees, and a vast plunging of water faced into the full and rising moon. It was the North America of the imagination of the eighteenth century, a place of the "noble savage" and the romantic grandeur of the earth. The thunder of the fall reverberated back from its encirclement of cliff and forest, seizing upon the spirit's awareness, and haunting and deserting the porches of the ears. It was there I was sure to hear the rossignol, the nightingale of the habitant, singing his folksong of the river. Now I would hear him from the trees a little back from the fall, now from the very bush in the amphitheater, and now and then as an echo and an answer from the direction of the fields.

As the night deepened, and the beautiful, the orbed moon swam higher in the noble and eighteenth century heaven, the birds came to an end of their singing: one would wait for a last music and hear no more, the last, poor, small, foolish head asleep now under its wing. Only the cataract remained to thunder in the wood, tumbling down in its moon-pale wreaths and veils and roaring away out of space and one's bemused consciousness like some audible overflowing of the stream of earthly time.

III

The skies have cleared this morning after a downpour of Laurentian rain which began in the very middle of the night, a small sigh of beginning rain abruptly turning into a pattering crepitation which deepened as suddenly into one immense and vehement roar. The first dawn was still grey but now the cloud mass is opening, and a bright midsummer day has the whole village in its keeping. On such a morning the farm country seems as mild and rustic as some small "pays" of the Île de France or Normandy. It is a French "cocorico!" which chanticleer here sounds from his pen —"Cocorico!" the boldest sound we ever hear, I think, of life self-justified and resolute, domestic yet cosmically undaunted. The village world has been quiet and at its breakfast, but now a wagon passes, scaring up a rats' nest of English sparrows from the puddles of the road, and past the window flies an iridescent tree swallow, a civil and pleasant bird and one of the first to return to this country in the spring.

In this advanced region of the north, plants must grow with a will once they are out of the ground, thrusting themselves, as it were, out of the furrow towards a sun who will not stay. The gardens grow fast, various plants taking on a new habit of growth, and towering up into stalks which are weedlike in their energy of life. It is now full midsummer on the river, the gardens are thriving, and in the fields by the road, as one goes through the village, a gay flowering of yellow buttercups, white daisies and purple vetch have made a Laurentian carpet of the grass. What of the birds of this open country between the spruce on the sky line and the hidden quiet of the glens? At first glance, the region does not seem a particularly rewarding field. Its birds are the birds of the higher but not extreme northeast and the birds you will see about a

farm in northern Maine, you will—for the most part—
see here. The same familiar kingbird crouches on these
Canadian wires, the same pretty goldfinch perches on
the seeding thistle and has therefrom his French name
"le chardonneret," and the same black crows rise caw-
ing from the fields and fly to cover before the darkening
wind and rain. Only yesterday while far up the hillside
of cleared land, a bobolink, la Goglu, went over the
fence rails and down the slopes towards the farms.
The northern birds are here, but to this one must add
a note that such birds are present in noticeably smaller
numbers than they are with us, and that various species
familiar to New England are here infrequent or unknown. The bluebird is one of these. He is known; he
has his French name—le rouge-gorge bleu—but he is a
chance and lovely apparition on these roads.

I note, in particular, a definite lack of orchard
birds. Apples grow here, and there is scarce an old farm
without a few embattled trees doing their best—but it
is not orchard country. I find myself wondering as to
the robin we see. The bird is not what he is with us.
Across the frontier, the robin is a household bird, a
builder on piazzas and in trees near the house, and his
song is a part of the life of early morning and the
lengthening peace of the midsummer afternoon. In this
region, I do not see robins near the houses, and I seldom
hear their song. Indeed, there are times when there
seem no robins at all. (It has been said that the bird is
noticeably less of a household creature in the northern
part of his range.) Perhaps it is a matter of two different strains. A number of ornithologists have long suspected that there are two robins in the northeast, or

to be more definite, two habitat groups, one a northern bird of the north forest and the farm frontier—such a bird as must have been known to the Indians, and a second bird, more southern in its range—which has adapted itself to the white man's way of life. According to this theory, it is the Canadian robin we see in our New England winters, the bird having come down to us from the Canadian forest, whilst the bird we see in summer, the household retainer and plump piazza-builder, is his southern kinsman come north to raise a family. Is it, then, the northern bird one sees on the Côte Nord a hundred and fifty and two hundred miles down the river from the Saguenay? The bird is there, and in wilderness country. And is it the Canadian robin some have seen in Maine, in the later depth of winter, living in small flocks in the coastal woods? Be the local bird what it is, I miss the morning song, the comic stride across the shadows under the elms, and the cocked head listening for the worm.

The hummingbird—le colibri—is entirely at home, visiting these Laurentian gardens with entire familiarity. An intrepid seafarer, he goes even farther, and crossing the Gulf of St. Lawrence, reaches the remote fishing villages of Newfoundland.

One land bird is the very spirit of the river. All up and down the St. Lawrence from Montreal to the gulf, swallows haunt the borders of the stream. As the valley darkens, and the summer sun vanishes in the clouds of the northwest, the birds come from all their cliffs and habitations, filling the evening light with their darting and skimming wings. They have a great liking for these old half-deserted wharves, perhaps because the loading of pulpwood attracts or releases insect life, and about them they gather in their twilight eagerness and haste, adding their living ecstasy to the eternal onrush of the darkening tides. Such birds are cliff swallows for the most part, and their colonies nest in the glacial fans of clay and gravel which occur along the stream.

To compensate for this lesser number of birds and birds by species, certain birds of the evergreen forest may be seen about the farms. There are always stands of native spruce about the grounds of older dwellings (kept there to act as barriers against the wind and snow) and it is to such trees that the kinglet comes, the tiny roitelet whom Dominion poets both French and English have celebrated as a bold Canadian. Both the ruby-crowned and the golden-crowned are residents, the first being locally the most familiar, and both nest in the farm spruces of the agricultural plateau. (I cannot recall ever having encountered the birds in the wilder country of the upland ridge.) There was a certain pleasant morning long ago, a part of a remembered autumn on the river, when I went walking in a wood of spruce to the south of the coastal road, losing myself half a dozen times on a path which had ceased to be a path, and coming suddenly to a glade in the wood beside a wilderness ravine. On one side, the spruce shone in the full silence and the sun, to the other lay the descent and a chilliness of shade. At the far end of the sunlit wall, there was a picture bird life such as I had never hoped to see. One tree was astir with kinglets; the tiny, lovely creatures climbing in and out of the spruce branchlets with an incessant and busy eagerness. Had the pretty ornaments on some great, old-fashioned Christmas tree suddenly become alive, and darted about among the candles, the effect could not have been more surprising, so similar was the scale of the flocklet and the sunlit branch thrust from its inner core of shade into the glisten of the sun. There was no singing, but the conversation of small "ksis" or "tsips" was like the chatter of a gathering in a room, a general social sound which had its own being apart from individual noise. Both species were at hand, in this instance the golden-crowned predominating. Friends tell me that this species sometimes winters in sheltered country near Quebec.

It was a charming sight to see such a stir of little hardy birds, and I had plenty of time to watch them on the tree. But, alas, somehow or other they presently became aware of me, and with a concerted rush were off into some hideaway of the deeper glens, leaving their Christmas tree only a spruce by the St. Lawrence standing with others in a wood.

IV

The country which stands above, hiding its distance behind the eternal spruce, is a kind of no man's land as it advances towards the farm. One ought to see and hear various small birds in that upland wood, but I have seen little and heard less. It is a various region, now wild and picturesque and threaded by streams which have each their nameless cataract, now little more than a tract of bush growing where the pulp exploitation has passed like a corrupt storm. I am told that old clearings are woodpecker regions, and that the red-

breasted grosbeak—le gros-bec à poitrine rose—is a familiar of the bush country a little farther back into the
north. To the casual wanderer, the most familiar of its
birds is the ruffed grouse, la gelinotte de Canada. Here
in the north the bird one sees appears to represent a
geographical race, for the plumage is far more grey than
anything I have ever seen over the border. So wild is
the back country that the bird has maintained itself
well in spite of heavy gunning, and there is scarce a
pilgrimage in the spruce without a sudden crash of
wings exploding in one's ears, and a feathery, diminu-
endo rush across the fragrant green and the region sense
of nonhuman loneliness.

So much for the coast and the transitional Canadian life-zone of which it is a part: what of the Hudsonian zone which lies behind? Beyond the "height of
land", the vast subarctic wilderness of mountain and
lonely forest has its own population. It is there you will
see the Canada jay as a common sight, and hear at night
the hunting owls. In the legends of the bush it is always
the great horned owl who is the genius and demon of
the forest, falling through the dusk as noiselessly as a
snowflake to clutch the fur hat of a returning lumber-
jack, and give poor Jean Baptiste the fright of his life.
What yells have been heard through a darkening wood!
I doubt if there is much relation—during summer—
between the two life-zones, though Hudsonian types
occasionally are to be seen on the Saguenay and about
the Lac St. Jean. (Only a year or two ago a young polar
bear wandering far out of his range and away from the
sea was shot in the St. Jean country.) Returning to
birds, the Laurentian National Park likewise has its

northerners, the Canada jay being one of the common-
est sights about its camps. A northerner surely, for the
bird—to quote Mr. Taverner—has been known to set
about incubating its eggs at a temperature thirty below
zero Fahrenheit.

It is out of this northern forest, out of these miles
of silence and advancing cold that the little, hardy winter birds come south to the open country and the river.
The returning warblers will pass almost unseen, trailing a paler sun to warmer earth and longer days: even
the snow buntings will press on, blowing like autumn
leaves over the great shining slopes to their favorite winter country on the sunlit side of "Chalore" bay. The
various grosbeaks, too, will pass and perhaps the strange
crossbills whom the habitant believes to be prophets
of some black intensity of cold. More and more snow,
more and more sleigh bells and red mufflers, and the
tiny red poll will be seen, perched on some branch out-
thrust from a drift and tearing at the frozen seed. And
some farmer walking by the shore will see a hunched,
white shape keeping watch on the broken, grinding,
churning mass of empty ice, the white owl come south
in winter through the arctic air and the iciclo brightness of the sun.

v

Far across the steely miles of the river, an earth
land and a cloud land of darkened blue, the south shore
of the widening estuary stands in a life-zone of quite
another kind. From Ontario to the transitional wilderness beyond the Saguenay the north of the river is, as

I have said, a part of the Canadian zone; to the south
the coast is transitional austral bounded in its own back
country by the reappearing Canadian zone of the high
forests of New Brunswick and New England. It is geo-
graphically a northeastern province, but the influence
of the west, of the lakes and the prairies, is concealed
in the milder scene, the earth tensions and currents of

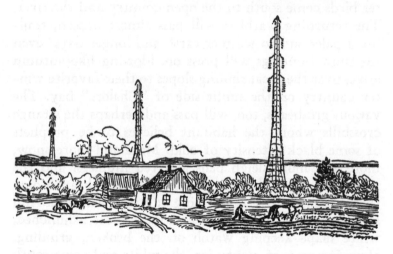

the great central valley flowing eastward along these
southern reaches towards the sea. Now and then, as if to
point the moral, birds of the Gulf coast, adventuring .
north along the Mississippi, turn seaward and find
themselves in the St. Lawrence east of Montreal. (An
ibis from Louisiana was a recent visitor to the southern
marshes of the Lac St. Pierre.) Quite apart from this
western and continental influence, the river is in itself
a most formidable biological barrier between southern
and northern kingdoms, halting all kinds of plants and

creatures at each shore. So be not deceived by appearances and similarities; until the Canadian zone leaps the river at the approaches to Gaspé, the whole south region is another world.

It is the south shore, and here are the birds one has been missing just across the river. Here they are, the robins and the brown thrashers, as one might see them on the Merrimac or the Piscataqua. The country, moreover, has lost its northern and mountain shadow, and miles of the actual bank have become as earthy and rural as any little slope overhanging a small New England stream. It is with a musing question that from such a place one's eye escapes to the huge St. Lawrence. In this strange rusticity there is water everywhere, brooks and rills seeping out of the earth bank towards the blue immensity below. The naturalist will now find himself again in shore-bird country, for these flats and tidal meadows have been prepared for those searching beaks and hurrying swift feet. (The hostile, tumbled rocks of the northern coves are not for such wanderers.) Walking through the meadows, I often scare up a flight of greater yellowlegs—le grand chevalier à pieds jaunes —and the wind brings me the sweet tremolo whistle of their call as they fall off into the dusk. Perhaps the most familiar of the shore-bird tribe is the spotted sandpiper—la maubêche tachetée. I find the birds on the open beach; I come upon them in the field country above. Only the other day, I remember, I startled a bird in the fields above, and instead of taking to its wings, it scurried into the shelter of the bush quite like a sort of marine bobwhite. It is a pretty creature, and the line of white through its eye is unusually clear.

I was once on this shore in such a country as I have described, and near a pretty spring overflowing from its pool below the bank. There was a village and a road somewhere above, but the beach was unvisited and still, no distant voice or footfall troubling its solitariness or the mild south wind. Behind me the earth bank was overgrown with hardwood bush in full midsummer leaf, and as it followed the coast it wavered and turned like an old city wall, making its little regions invisible one from the other: only the great river moving direct and free into the east. I remember that it was early in the morning, somewhere between six and seven o'clock, and the sun was in the sky south of the wall. Far across, the Laurentians faced the morning, so far away that houses and villages were lost in the mountain slopes, the heights returning from an association with man back to the elemental earth and their stupendous continents of mist. The place had so lovely a mood of earth and was so pleasant and withdrawn that I lingered awhile beside the spring. Becoming thus myself a part of the quiet and the mood, I presently saw that the small birds of the region had long ago discovered the overflowing rill. A sparrow had flown away as I approached, and presently to the water came a male chewink who fluttered in out of nowhere, drank, and hid again. Much later came a pair of yellow warblers who monopolized the pool with entire fearlessness, hopping about and fluttering, to be gone, too, in their time.

It was a pleasant experience thus to see small birds at their own spring and in their own world, to see the characteristic gestures and gaits, the suspicions and alerts, and the completely natural, the pretty attitudes.

I kept at some distance from the scene, not wishing to intrude myself within the borders of its awareness, and was glad to see how untroubled the visitors bent their small heads to the living water. When the yellow warblers had flown, I went nearer, and saw how the marge of the pool was all overprinted with a cross-hatching of many tiny feet. When I returned later in the morning, the beach was still empty and the sun had risen above the bank. There were no birds at the pool, but as I watched I heard stirrings above me in the leaves, and from beyond, some small and half-remembered song.

CHAPTER FIFTEEN

Indian Pilgrimage

IN CERTAIN of its aspects, a journey beside the great St. Lawrence is an adventure beyond politics and frontiers into the older America of the forest, the cataract, and the shadow of trees, an adventure into the pages of *The Last of the Mohicans*, and within sound of the grave and romantic voices talking in the immemorial quiet of the woods. It is something of a pilgrimage, too, into the America of the late eighteenth and early nineteenth century colorists and engravers where the Indian and his wife and a child stand by a forest stream and a red-coated soldier bargains for a trinket sewn with beads. What a blessed quiet reigns in such old scenes, drawn before the age of violence and squalor had emerged from the hands of the Devil, its father! One can almost hear a leaf fall, touching other fallen leaves with a last delicate scratch of sound, or the purling of the brook flowing with such sylvan decorum through the glade. It is to the artists of Britain that we owe the preservation of such charming and old-fashioned glimpses of the older continent, for the young men from London were touched by the landscapes in its virginal and mysterious splendor and crossed the Atlantic to paint it in Canada, returning home with canvases and water colors which the great engravers and printers of mezzotints made popular in the ceremonious Geor-

gian world. Indeed, to this very day, in the windows
of those print shops just to one side of Piccadilly,
Niagara still plunges green and white in its eighteenth
century sublimity, whilst the Indian and the redcoat,
enclosed in a portfolio, wait but a request to revisit the
London day.

Always the Indian; of that figure every nation and
indeed every age has had its dream. The romance of the
American Indian is a part of the history of the Western
mind. It is worthy of note that it was not the Indian
of the great barbaric civilizations to the south, not the
Aztec noble or the Peruvian in his woven mantle, who
captured the world's imagination, but the wild man to
the north, the tawny hunter in his moccasins, the
painted savage crouching by the fire. The first lines of
the composite figure show us the Algonquin of the
coast, the pencil sketching-in a picturesque figure coming to greet strangers with a certain ceremoniousness
and a natural turn for trading and sociability, a first
portrait which the bitter struggles and massacres to
come never quite erased from European memory. The
Jesuits of France and Canada are the next to work from
life, being the first Europeans to know the northern
"Indian" from intimate association with his flea-bitten
dogs and smoke-filled lodges. Here the lines are less
favorable, the truly heroic pages of the *Relations* de-
picting an Iroquoian primitive for whom the fathers
would have enthusiastically pre-empted Mr. Kipling's
famous "half devil and half child." Appalling as was the
life portrayed, seeming even now a mixture of the
Stone Age and hell, the accounts brought the "Indian"
out more clearly, and succeeded in touching with power

the imagination and the piety of France. Thus little by little the figure takes shape, character and light and shade adding themselves to the drawing, till presently that honorable dream, the noble savage, comes with dignity from the painted forest and the rainbow on Niagara.

That a child of nature, a creature of the instinctive self and the untutored mind, should be a noble being is surely a dream which does honor to the imaginative soul of man. The idea conceals a certain criticism of civilization, for if the man of the woods could be such a fine fellow, of what use was the world's baggage of institutions and forms? Yet the most interesting thing about the noble savage (which has been too little remarked upon) is the fact that, to a notable degree, the figure was real. The noble savage was noble and he was a savage. The Stone Age Iroquoian primitive had in a scant hundred years crossed the astronomical abyss between the Neolithic and the age of Louis Quinze. What primitive people have ever done as much in a century of history? The Jesuit fathers would have scarcely known their man. This is the figure which so moved Franklin and Benjamin West; this is the chieftain and warrior with his gorget of silver and his blanket of finest London wool; this is Uncas as both ideal and human being. What is unreal is not the figure but the Nature out of which he comes. It is the Nature of literary convention, the Nature of contemporary literature, an image of the gardens of Versailles and St. James's Park, the intense thread of violences and cruelties having been sentimentally removed from the formal and pompous tapestry. Yet look again at the figure brushing

aside the blue-green and woven leaves, a circular crown
of feathers on his head; wait but another moment, and
the tapestry boughs will presently melt into the great
eighteenth century trees of Pennsylvania, and the figure, changing and drawing near, be seen as flesh and
blood.

With the eighteenth century passing of the Indian
as a political force, the eighteenth century "Indian,"
feathers and all, dissolves out of life to live on in literature. Of the noble savage presently only the dream remained. (Thanks to Cooper, entranced adolescents were
to read of him in every European tongue.) To exist in
reality, the figure had to be free to be an Indian, the
Stone Age and the eighteenth century managing some
kind of picturesque and happy blend. Encircled after
the Revolution by the hunger and advancing pressure
of the whites, the Indian of the east shrank back to the
last meager relics of his lands, no longer defending them
by arms but by contests of law. Through the open windows of courthouses built in the Greek revival manner,
the sonorous oratory of Indian chieftains in blue broadcloth and silver buttons floated out into a world whose
quiet the first railroad engines were presently to disturb
with a first imperious bell. So began the new times, the
long years of powerlessness, estrangement, and unher-
alded fortitude. The Algonquin of the coast, the seventeenth century Indian was gone. He existed, he had his
tiny islets and even a village or two almost all his own,
but the pressure of the surrounding world had weak-
ened his hold on his own way of life, and he was only
too often a basket-selling ghost in a Daniel Webster hat.
In this state of Maine, in the early nineteenth century,

small family bands sometimes came to ask leave to camp in some wooded cove of a favorite lake, and would spend the summer there, an open fire twinkling at night on the beach by the canoes. In the autumn gift was returned for gift, and on some late September night when Capella was rising higher over the cleared rye-fields and the first farms, some friend would look from a kitchen window and see no fire on the shore.

It is the western Indian who today holds first place in most imaginations, an artistic and archaeological interest in the Pueblos beginning to fade out the Indian horseman of the plains. Of more vivid times, the western war bonnet alone remains, and this the eastern Indian has adopted as a kind of racial uniform, wearing it as others wear a lapel pin or an elk's tooth. (He would look more himself with his one eagle's feather.) I have seen but do not know this western survival, for a passer-by, even a winter's visitor, is less than a cloud shadow in so ancient and continuing a world. My own interest remains with the Algonquins, with my neighbors of the coast and the northeast, with the men and women of the narrow paths of the great forest rolling eastward from the mountains to the sea. Those who have not seen you, oh friends, following such a path in your swift and beautiful sureness, your feet and the earth united in a mystery of oneness and quiet, will never understand how much a part you are of the land from which you spring! And beautiful as are the Indian arts of the west, I prefer those made here, with the sea and the forest in their making. Incomparable in its rightness and perfection as a fine abstract design may be, the fierce desert light making an eternal high noon

on the side of pot or jar, such designs often conceal
a flight from life in that the lines are the final and un-
recognizable formula of something that has life and
being. Such a perfection of the abstract joins hands
with mathematics and the nonhuman, and the art of
its inspiration has often no more humanity and warmth
than a quadratic equation. With due respect for the
creation of symbols and ultimate simplicities, I prefer
a bird to be something a little else than the square root
of minus one.

Our Indian arts of the higher northeast are far
more primitive, and represent the crafts of a hunter
people living a primitive and nomadic life. Each little
gathering made what it needed, and humanized the
thing made with some simple decoration. Birchbark and
porcupine needles, basket strips of the white ash, bone,
spruce root, sinew, hide and stone—there was so little
to work with. The birchbark, however, lent itself inter-
estingly to design, creating a style which was all its own
of silhouettelike figures of the larger forest animals.
Limited as were its materials and various the nature of
its design, what one feels in the art is an essential humanity. It is as near nature and as much a part of nature as the print of a foot beside a pool. And once these
simpler peoples had been introduced to European beads
and technics, they evolved an art whose sense of color
and floral design is in itself a unique flowering of the
human spirit.

The eighteenth century had moved on: the nineteenth was daily taking shape as the white man's very
own. The continent was his where he chose to go. So
complete was the victory across the more temperate and

exploitable latitudes that the invader himself forgot
that the continent was greater than the shadow of his
hand. Beyond the noise of his industries and the over-
flow of his power waterfalls, beyond the steely tenor
of the circular saw greedily destroying the great archaic
forest, beyond the seas which remained open in winter
and beyond their skies, the immense American north,
almost half the continent, remained as a shelter for the
past. Inaccessible and cold, too short of summer for the
plough and too rocky for the furrow, its timber spin-
dling out to the vast wastes of the barrens, the north
invited neither conquest nor conqueror. It was a wilderness, a thing with its own primeval devils, a solitude
curving up over the earth from the waters of the St.
Lawrence to the pole. It had belonged to the Indian
in the prehistoric past, his it would remain. More than
any other part of the continent it is still his today. Only
in that vast nothingness will you find the red man (and
I speak here of the Algonquin of the forest) without
that mask those of us who have shared his lodges know
he wears when our white world has enclosed him and
turned the key, that mask which no word of his be-
trays of a concealed, patient, and reflective hopelessness.
In the north the landscape is still Indian, and Canadian
liners on the homeward run, entering the noble strait
of Belle Isle, see to the west the austere and unpeopled
coast of the first discoverers.

Behind that rim of surges there are none to hear;
beyond that first meager and twisted wall of the forest,
live the Montagnais and the Nascapi, kindred people,
the northernmost of the Algonquins. Farther west, in
the thousand upon a thousand miles to the north of the

lakes, dwell the Chippewas and the roving Crees, the short, dark people of the higher wilderness. The whole vast region is under the authority of the white man's law, administered with justice and power, but the earth forces of the wilderness are archaic and hostile, having as little to do with law and the white spirit as a billow of sleet in a gale. It is the Indian's America.

II

The St. Lawrence had turned into a sea. Eastward lay a seeming ocean and an horizon; to the south, the last blue island of the south shore had vanished below the curve of water and the earth. Spreading out our charts on deck, we estimated that the northern tributary into whose river mouth we were bound lay about two-thirds of the way eastward from Quebec to the opening of the gulf, and it was near. Appearing with inconsequential suddenness, a red church presently came into a view across the water of an opening bay, and a line of small, unpainted houses projected itself between sea and sky on the August afternoon. It was Bersimis, the large village of the Montagnais Indians of the Côte Nord. The water began to discolor with the forest brownness of the fresh, inflowing stream. Rounding a great horn of river sand, and exchanging our sea eyes and consciousness for the restored perspectives of the shore, we drew up to a large wharf on the tributary.

Looking about, I thought to myself that Indian settlements in the north have all of them a family identity. There is sure to be a church, a store or two, a trading post of a fur company, the quarters of the government officials, and the scattered, unpainted shacks of the Indians. Sometimes there are tents beyond the houses: there were none here. At Bersimis, as in other places, the community stood isolated against the wilderness, a rendezvous of human beings holding their own between the empty horizons of the river and the gaunt and final wall of the north woods.

I had heard of the village from various friends. It was difficult to reach by either land or sea. The last road in the northeast ended at Portneuf beyond the Saguenay, leaving the real wilderness to stare at you across the Portneuf River, and Bersimis was at least forty miles beyond. One visitor had followed the telegraph line through the bush. The only boat to make calls, slowing up off the village once or twice a month, started from a port far down the opposite shore. In winter government planes brought mail and attended to emergencies. The best way to get there would be to hire a fishing boat or a heavy launch somewhere beyond the Saguenay.

There were also permits to be secured, for the village was protected by the government. Once there, however, I would see something of Algonquin life, for the Montagnais of Bersimis were probably the largest Indian tribal group left anywhere in the high northeast. They were descendants of the hunting, nomad tribes who had once held the wild country to the north of the St. Lawrence, often venturing far westward through the bush. The community was still a part of early nineteenth century Indian life; in the twentieth, it lived by the fur trade. The Indians arrived on the river in early summer and spent two or three months at Bersimis in quarters built for them by the government. At Bersimis they made their contact with religion and civilization, got married in church, had their children baptized, attended to their religious duties and sold their furs. At the close of the short northern summer each family group packed its canoe with flour, tea, lard and ammunition and returned to the bush above the height of land. Here the tribe dispersed, breaking up into family bands in the ancient Algonquin manner, each band having its own hunting and trapping area. They lived in the bush in shelters or tents, and there was often only a wall of canvas between the newborn child and the arctic gale.

When spring—which is the bad, the hated season in the woods—had come to an end with its mud and rotten ice, and the tributary rivers were free, the families came out of the woods in their canoes, each with its bale of pelts. Sometimes the luck had been good and they soon had money to spend; sometimes the luck had been bad, and men, women and children had a thin time. Some families had better luck than others. The aged and the ill were left behind at Bersimis where the sisters wintered them in a sort of hospital-home and also kept a school. The Fudist fathers were in charge of the parish, and the resident government agent—by a convention frequent in Canada—was also a physician.

The tribe was large, and there were sometimes five or six hundred Indians in the summer community. They kept one great annual feast and celebration, the Feast of the Assumption of the Virgin, which falls on August 15th. The celebration marked the traditional date of the return to the woods. Paddling from the St. Lawrence into the brown wash of the Betsiamis, the people had set out together in a fleet, and there had been shouting and calling out of good-byes till they turned a headland of the lesser river. Almost a year would elapse before they would be seen again, places empty in some canoes, and the children in arms staring at the red church tower and the beach.

III

One knows nothing whatever about a people until one has seen a number of them together. A common consciousness has to come into being before any group is free to act in its own pattern and mood. The first Indian I saw was watching us land at the wharf. Indian villages are apt to include a native comic or acknowledged jester, and I judged this first Indian to be the man. He was short, hardly taller than a stocky boy just out of grammar school, and his alert eyes were full of mischief and curiosity in his brown Indian face. Taking us all in, he tossed a disconnected word or two of French upon the air, all by way of identification of us, greeting, and humor. Whites seldom apprehend the Indian capacity for humor, for elfish, often ironic fun. They are thoroughly capable, for instance, of "playing Indian" exactly like small boys when they feel that it is expected of them by visiting whites. I found later in the day that I was not mistaken in my identification. This was the Tyl Eulenspiegel of the tribe.

The last population of Indians I had seen gathered into a large community had been that of a pueblo on the Rio Grande. I remembered a morning in the spring, a great dance before a row of cottonwoods, and the strange, yet curiously beautiful orange-brown color of the smooth half-naked bodies crouching and treading to the ritual measure of the drum. Here in the north, the forest made for no such color or sleekness. Passing us by in the early afternoon, coming towards us between their unpainted shacks, the Algonquin Montagnais turned to us faces as dark brown as dark, old-fashioned, plug tobacco. The eye, again, was brown, but of a deep and lively glisten, having nothing of that obsidian remoteness which can be stony in the west. As a people, they were neither tall nor short, but of a certain lean, well-proportioned middle height, and they walked with the Indian assurance which has its roots in the old connection with the earth. Now and then, stockier, heavier types brought out the more conventional spareness. The clothes were simply habitant French Canadian—slouch hat, blue windbreaker jacket and bottes sauvages. A few were wearing new-looking woolen shirts of the large black-and-white and red-and-black checks popular in the north. The women, however, more conservative, had retained something Indian and characteristic. It was the picturesque and handsome Montagnais squaw hat, a kind of modified liberty cap affair, cut full at the bottom like a bag and narrowing to a somewhat mounded top. To make it, tapering segments of broadcloth, alternately red and black, had been sewn together to a peak which was worn falling over towards the forehead. Around the base, looking very Chinese, ran a decorative piping of colored silks very finely rolled together—a Montagnais handicraft.

The hair was worn in a kind of roll over the ear, the arrangement just showing below the edge of the hat.

The beginnings of such a hat are surely European in their inspiration—for the first Montagnais had no cloth—but the Indian mind has made the design its own and the whole effect is ritual and Asiatic. It has nothing whatever to do with Cartier or Champlain, but much to do with Marco Polo and the Grand Chan. Adding to the effect was the power and dignity of the faces of many of the older women. The patient, dark, Asiatic visages were not "beautiful" in the formal and European sense of the word, but they had that compensation of age in a primitive society, a look of character and realized authority.

One could tell the worldly circumstances of a family by the look of the dogs outside the door. Where the family had done well at its hunting and trading, the dogs looked comfortable; where the family was hard put to it, the dogs had the household's lean and hungry air. The board houses had a kitchen and a bedroom and were furnished with few things. In a kitchen you would find a small wood range, a table, a chair or two, a dish or two, an iron pot, a devotional calendar, and scarce another item of property. The list, perhaps, sounds barren, but one felt nowhere a need of things. The rooms were neat, and there was a complete naturalness and ease in the austerity. But I must not forget the bit of caribou hide which served so many as a mat, nor the home-mounted caribou horns with the one old hat hanging from a prong.

In front of the presbytery stood a garden walled about with straggling wire. It was August and the short

summer really over, but there were raspberries still
waiting to be picked in the enclosure, one last grim
rose, and noble clumps of aconite in early flower. As
I sat alone on the presbytery steps in the dusk, staring
down into the garden, and fending off the wilderness
mosquitoes, there came towards me from behind the
presbytery two Indian men. One was in old blue clothes
and high boots, the other in old clothes more grayish,
and I thought them both to be younger men in the thirties. Some sort of strange motion and scuffle as of dogs,
yet not quite doglike, was going on behind them, and I
presently saw that the visitor in blue had with him two
bear cubs on a long chain borrowed from a trap. The
little bears were both fretful and mischievous, weaving
about and pulling back, but the Indian leader chivied
them along, and I saw him fasten the pair to a post of
the presbytery stairs. The visitors then came over to
me, and seeing that they wished to speak, I made signs
to them to join me on the steps and so we sat close together in the dusk. Their faces were very dark and
Indian above the poorish European clothes, but they
were not, thank God, smashed men, and the look on
their youngish faces was unhaunted and completely
natural. The bear leader began by speaking into his
companion's ear a long sentence in Montagnais. When
this interesting and mysterious communication had
come to its end, the companion turned his head to me
and translated the message into easy French.

"The chief has come to make you welcome," he
said. "He is glad you have come to visit us and hopes
you will stay."

"Tell the chief I thank him very much," I said

(and here I translate my French reply). "A stranger will long remember such a welcome in his heart. Tell him that I have heard of him and of his people, and am glad to be with them at Bersimis."

This seemed to please them, and we parted with an old-fashioned and pleasantly ceremonial politeness which was both Indian and French. (It was the beginning of a friendship.) Standing on the steps, I watched them unloose their cubs, and turn the corner of the house. In their winterish clothes, the visitors melted swiftly into the night. It had grown cold and dark.

IV

In its make-up, Bersimis remained a genuine Indian town. Including the missionary priests at the presbytery, the government agent and his family, the two young men at the Hudson's Bay post, the Royal Canadian Mounted Police officer, and a lesser official and his family, there were only some twenty or thirty whites at the village as opposed to five or six hundred Montagnais. The three fathers (my most kind and hospitable hosts) were priests of the Eudist order, a missionary body dedicated to carrying on difficult work. Two of the fathers worked with the Indians, Father Denis Doucet, head of the mission, being in charge at Bersimis, Father Luc Sirois having the care of the Indian settlement at the Pointe aux Outardes, whilst the third missionary, Le Père Arthur Gallant, had charge of the colonists established here and there along the coast. The Montagnais language is a specialized and rather difficult dialect of Algonquin, but Father Doucet and Father Sirois spoke it with the easiest fluency. The Indians were very proud of their abilities. "Ah—you should hear the fathers speak," they would say. "They are as good as we are; they miss nothing."

Contrariwise, when the Montagnais spoke French, it was spoken exceedingly well. (Only a few, however, had any knowledge of the tongue.) I remember one Montagnais woman saying to us in as crisp and well-articulated French as I have ever heard—she speaking with humor—"Yes, we go back and forth between the woods and the river just like the animals. C'est curieux, but when any of the people have to spend the winter on the river, they are sick all the time. When we are in the woods nobody has even a cold."

The morning of the Feast of the Assumption began with a cheerless light and a look of rain coming. As the Montagnais take the weather of their feast day to be something of an omen of the luck of the coming year, this promised but ill. Moreover, if it rained, there would be no procession at all. From the presbytery steps, the cloud which covered the entire sky seemed as unmoving as the earth itself, a pall of melancholy and grey fixed above the wilderness and the rivers: only a little listless air moving along the shore.

Under such skies, the ceremonies of the day began with a high mass and a wedding. The whole tribe was at hand, the small world of dark and ancient people meeting together in the church. For the most part, the men seemed to be arriving by themselves or along with other men; the women coming in their own time with the small children of the family. The great bell was

still ringing as we climbed the stairs to our places in
the organ loft beside the Indian choir, the muffled swing
and clang thundering out close overhead as if to sum-
mon all that was of human in the north. A young Indian tugged at the rope, another, scarce a grown youth,
sat at the organ keys, and whispering with decorum
in Montagnais and discussing their Latin hymns, the
singers consulted with each other in the manner of all
choirs. Below us, divided by the length of the middle
aisle, the sexes sat apart. A quiet sea of bright, parti-
colored caps marked the women, another sea of black
Indian heads the men and older boys. Now began high
mass, the great ritual of the Roman West, served by
little Indians in red soutanes and white surplices, and
somehow entering with the benediction of the altar
and the three fathers in their feast-day robes, appeared
the Indian bride and groom. A seat of honor, a sort
of small parlor sofa, had been placed for them in the
chancel directly below the altar, and there side by side
they sat down in nuptial decorum to share and follow
the feast-day mass.

Both were young. From where we sat looking
down, the slim girl might have stepped into the church
from any school or office. In contrast to the older
women in their native caps and bulks of Sunday black,
the bride was wearing (one must not escape that in-
escapable phrase) a little suit of light blue, a light-blue
coat with sleeves cut in the modern manner, and dark
shoes with French heels. With this went a small straw
hat of the year's mail-order fashion, indeed the entire
costume had undoubtedly been ordered from the
French edition of Eaton's catalogue. The groom was

dressed in a good, mail-order blue with long trousers, and wore black city shoes. It was all a picture to remember forever as a part of one's experience—the mass at the depth of the scene in its splendor of incense, vestments and immemorial gesture, the Indian boys in their Catholic surplices, the bride and groom in their catalogue clothes, and the congregation in its decorum and dark attention.

After the service, I encountered the bride and groom on the presbytery piazza, talking there with Father Doucet, their priest. The groom I took to be in his early twenties, but young Indians are not young with our kind of youth. They take on manhood with the directness of a simpler world. The bride in her blue costume seemed very shy, the groom more at ease; neither was at home in French.

"I suppose you will soon be going to the woods," I said, reflecting on the blue coat and the French heels. (Where would they be put away?) The pleasant young man nodded and smiled.

"Yes, they'll go with the others," said Father Doucet in French. "I understand he has bought a new tent to begin housekeeping. They are both good young people." He then added something in Montagnais, and the married pair went in to sign the book.

v

It was noon. The sky was still one cloud, and though rain threatened every moment, not a drop had fallen. The village seemed very quiet. Every now and then at the presbytery one of the fathers would go to the door to study the sky and the listless wind. The Indians were doing the same thing, outside their own doors, looking up to the unchanging immensity of cloud. They would not hazard their cherished image of the Virgin in a grey St. Lawrence rain. At two o'clock, one looking up would have seen for a while a paler wanness overhead, a second darkening, and then a first grey brightening vaguely luminous with the covered sun. Beyond the somber purple of the garden aconites, the darkness to the south remained unchanged, a gloom of cloud vast and tenebrous above the paler waters of the estuary.

Yet there fell no rain. As the hour of the procession approached, the chief and the fathers of the mission came together in one last consultation to study the half-threat, half-promise overhead. The sky was certainly brighter than it had been an hour before. The talk at an end, I saw the chief walk briskly away, and in a few minutes the church bell began to ring.

The decision had been made, and announced to the tribe. Starting from some near-by house, a few first arrivals were already going to the church. Now came more and more still, men, women and children, a spirit of Indian seriousness on every dark face . . . the organ playing in the church and the bell steadily ringing. Presently arrived some ten young Indian men in blue Sunday clothes similar to those worn by the groom at the wedding, each man carrying a shotgun which he carefully stacked in a corner of the vestibule. Our friend the handsome young police officer was also at hand, wearing his dress uniform with its fine scarlet tunic, and carrying his swagger stick; alert and quiet, he swiftly checked the guns. Last of all, accompanied by his mother, came a small child on crutches, a little Indian boy wanly pale under his brown Indian skin, who passing me by smiled up to me with the most touching and beautiful smile I have seen or ever will see on the face of a child. Oh Virgil, oh lacrimae rerum!

I had been told that the service in the church was short and I would best see the beginning of the procession if I waited by the presbytery. Some change of sound, some curious vibration across the psychic air, and I knew that the twenty minutes were at an end. The first to emerge from the church were the young men who had arrived with guns. On their dark faces shone a kind of a wild intentness, a look of purpose and readiness which was both primitive and eager, yet they did not hurly-burly down the steps, but came down properly with their pieces, and dividing into two groups, stationed themselves to each side of the walk. The scarlet tunic, too, was there, and checked the loading. Then came music from within the door, and with it a first pair of young Indian men carrying the forward poles of the Virgin's litter on their shoulders, then the Patroness herself standing above them in a bower of crepe paper blue and white—a small image, perhaps four feet high—then two more young bearers with the same solemnity and prideful fierceness and then, following in a great, slow company and walking two by two, the men of Bersimis.

At the foot of the steps, the young men raised their guns. A moment more, and a ragged volley of tribute and exultation saluted the Virgin passing in solemnity from her church into the native and roofless air. It was then I saw for the first time how lovely was the figure carried so triumphantly and religiously on high. The Virgin of Bersimis was no modernity of plaster and bad taste, but a charming old figure of the late eighteenth or early nineteenth century from some workshop of Catholic France, a real Queen of Heaven carved from

wood, and given a court splendor of painted robes of old gilt and late Renaissance brocade. Her hands were open in the immemorial gesture of the pitying and welcoming Mother, and with inclined head she came forth into her village and to her dark people, a queen wearing her crown.

A road stood at the end of the church walk, through grass and trodden dust following the beach of the St. Lawrence. Into this turned the procession, walking slowly to the east. Now came the women of the tribe, walking in twos close behind the men, their red-and-black caps a living brightness of color in the day's grey, half-reassuring gleam. Saving the scarlet tunic, who was somewhere else, the white laity of the community next closed in—officials and traders, boatmen and telegraphers, the little separate world of the stranger who had taken the inheritance. By twos we walked and at the Indian pace, watching the procession ahead turning the corner and the Virgin advancing upheld against the sky; the fathers in their robes, the little Indian acolytes, and all the village following. Soon we were all of us on the path beside the river, the empty beach below us and the immense sea of the St. Lawrence for the pale level of the world.

A quarter of a mile beyond the church, the village came to an end, a last Indian house turning a grey side to the wilderness and to the St. Lawrence ever widening. At this beginning of the forest and the end of what had been made human, the road, too, came to a close, having nowhere else to go. Over a dwarfed and encroaching scrub of northern bush this last of the village commanded a noble view of the river, and there, out of the last wild grass and dust, rose a Calvaire of the French-Canadian kind. The nailed and pendant image was fixed with its back to the forest, the melancholy head and circlet of thorn turned upon the vast horizons of the stream. It was an Indian Christ, its body painted darker, perhaps, by some Indian hand, and cross and figure had long been out of doors and weathered by the rain.

As in a sacred mystery, the Mother approached the Son. Some kind of little stand had been built near the cross, and on this the bearers rested the litter they had carried with such pride. There was silence now awhile, a kind of universal quiet of the human spirit and the mood of the great river and the earth, and then out of the silence came the voice of the priest raised in the beginning of a prayer and sending us all to our knees. It was beginning to darken again. Above the kneeling village and the sonorous Latin, above the murmuring of responses and the answering signs of the cross, Mother and Son alone remained exalted, the two figures raised above us in symbolic remembrance against the river and the sky. At the close of the prayer, a few light drops began to fall.

A few drops, but it did not rain. Not till the village had returned to the church with its Patroness was there a first shower. The Virgin of Bersimis in her robes and crown was then safe at home again.

Their Patroness once more enshrined, the village prayer said, and the annual blessing sought and given, the connection of the tribe with the St. Lawrence was broken, was ended for the year. Now the forest again lay ahead, the winter hunting and the snow, the iron pots of caribou meat, the boiling cups of English tea, and the terrible nights of the black, unhuman cold. The Indians would begin going the next morning, paddling their canoes into the brown current of the Betsiamis flowing freely from the north.

They were not alone in their farewell to the St. Lawrence; it was my own time to turn aside. The first frosts of autumn and September would presently be sharp in the mountains to the south, and the road so often followed from one sky to another, from one nation to the other nation must have its homeward and familiar way. Another month, and on the St. Lawrence sudden squalls of snow would drift strangely and fiercely among the bright-colored leaves from whose shelters the even brighter warblers had long ago withdrawn. To the south, beyond the hills, the cold northwest wind would shake the blue lakes to a daylong coursing of complaining waves, and in the quiet morning, the loon would be heard again from the cove hidden away behind the hill. Farewell, great river, on whose shores I have known so many a kindness, stream of the towering clouds and the paths of cloud reflected, of church bells heard, and of high paths followed in the hills, river of the northern rain, the spruce forest, and the solitary ranges, farewell, river of the northern sun.

Words by Thomas Moore
Old French Folk Tune

THE CANADIAN BOAT SONG
(From "Songs of the Rivers of America," edited by Carl Carmer with music arranged by Dr. Albert Sirmay.)

Brightly

1. Faint - ly as tolls the ev'- ning chime, Our voic- es keep tune and our oars keep time, __ Our voic- es keep tune and our oars keep time; Soon as the woods on shore look dim, We'll sing at St. Ann's our part - ing hymn; Row, broth - ers, row, the stream runs fast, The ra - pids are near and the day - light's past, The ra - pids are near and the day - light's past,

2. Why should we yet our sail un - furl? There is not a breath the blue wave to curl, __ There is not a breath the blue wave to __ curl; But when the wind blows off __ the shore, Oh! sweet - ly we'll rest the wear - y oar; Blow, breez - es, blow, the stream runs fast, The ra - pids are near and the day - light's past, The ra - pids are near and the day - light's past,

Index

INDEX 269

Forests (*Continued*)
pulpwood, 147-155, 183
scrub, of Côte Nord ("the bush"), 177
in winter, 31-33, 42
Forts, fur trade, 80, 82
France, 11, 50, 51
Revolution, 88-90, 102
Seven Years' War, 50-75
War of the Spanish Succession, 35
(*See also* French Canada)
Franklin, Benjamin, 242
Fraser's Highlanders, 68
Frederick the Great, 49, 51
Freighters, lake, 6
French Canada, 11, 18, 23
attitude toward earth, 107
and captives of Indians, 36-48
churchgoing, 163, 164
civilization within British dominion, 19, 92-94, 108, 109, 167
colonists, 177-184
cooking, 159, 160
dancing, 166
explorers, 115
forces influencing, 116, 117
habitants, 173-176, 251
houses, 97-109, 157-161
kitchens, 157
legends, 121-146
literature, 168
old, 88-109
painting and music, 41, 169
politics, 169, 174
religion, 106, 107
social gaiety, 108
songs, 94, 105, 109, 120, 123, 149, 180
Sunday, 156-166

French Canada (*Continued*)
veillée, 137, 166
villages, 11-14, 60, 75, 172
voyageurs, 79-87, 123, 128
(*See also* Clergy; Farming; France; Fur trade)
French Revolution, 88-90, 102
French West India Islands, 99
Frostbite, 27
Fur trade, 23, 34, 76-87, 132, 134, 203, 247-249
forts and stations, 76, 80, 82
French voyageurs, 79-87, 123, 128
revived by Scots, 76, 77

G

Galeries, 156, 160, 164-166
Ganoid, 215
Gallant, Arthur, Père, 255
Gaspé, 60, 237, 261
Georgian Bay, 81
Glen country, 222, 223, 226-229
Goldfinch, 230
Grand Portage, 81
Gray, Thomas, "Elegy," 67
Great Britain, 4
artists, 240, 241
fleet, 50, 59, 60, 63, 75
New France, conquest of, 16, 53-75, 118
officers, 74, 91, 95-98
seamanship, 181
Seven Years' War, 50-75
Great horned owl, 234
Great Lakes, fur stations, 76, 81
shipping, 113
Great Trace, 80, 81
Greater snow goose, 204
Greenland, 204

The Fraser

Reissue

The late BRUCE HUTCHISON
Introduction by VAUGHN PALMER

"One of the most soul satisfying books I have ever read, about one of the most exciting rivers I have ever seen." —Alfred C. Ames, *Chicago Tribune*

In *The Fraser*, Bruce Hutchison—one of Canada's great storytellers—relates the epic saga of the river whose history is one with that of British Columbia and her people. Hutchison's masterful narrative draws in the reader with its tale of gold rush and fur trade, heroism and despair. Vivid and exciting, *The Fraser* is a dramatic portrait of Canada's colourful past.

Paperback | 378 pages | 5.5 x 8.5" | 9780195438925

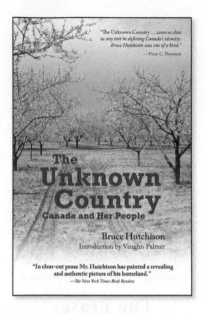

The Unknown Country
Canada and Her People
Reissue

The late BRUCE HUTCHISON
Introduction by VAUGHN PALMER

"*The Unknown Country* . . . came as close as any text in defining Canada's identity. Bruce Hutchison was one of a kind." —Peter C. Newman

 Governor General's Literary Award for Non-fiction

For an entire generation of Canadians, *The Unknown Country* defined their nation. It is a book that speaks to us still. Winner of the Governor General's Literary Award for Non-fiction, acclaimed by critics at home and abroad, this book presents an unforgettable portrait of a nation in the making—a portrait as vivid, lively, and true as when it first appeared during the dark, heroic days of the Second World War.

Paperback | 400 pages | 5.5 x 8.5" | 9780195438918

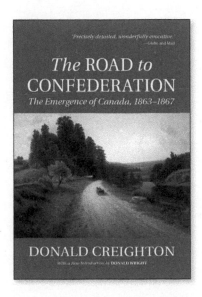

The Road to Confederation
The Emergence of Canada, 1863–1867
Reissue

The late DONALD CREIGHTON
Introduction by DONALD WRIGHT

"A happy, nostalgic celebration of the people and the process that had made Canadian federal union; precisely detailed, wonderfully evocative."—*Globe and Mail*

Donald Creighton was for many years one of Canada's foremost historians, a firm believer that history was closer to art than it was to science. Marked by beautiful, carefully crafted prose, *The Road to Confederation* reflects a style that perhaps no contemporary historian would dare: romantic, suspenseful, fearlessly narrative, and full of unapologetic opinions. It is a fascinating exploration of the personalities, the political logjams, even the debt problems that marked the period leading to Confederation.

Paperback | 544 pages | 6 x 9" | 9780195449211

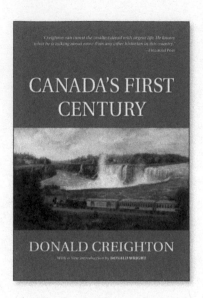

Canada's First Century
Reissue

The late DONALD CREIGHTON
Introduction by DONALD WRIGHT

"Creighton can invest the smallest detail with urgent life. He knows what he is talking about more than any other historian in this country."—*Financial Post*

Canada's First Century paints a large and complex canvas of historical rise and fall: a great transcontinental nation is built, but it is eventually undone as Canada turns its back on the British Empire and embraces a continental role alongside the United States. A courageous and contentious book for its day— Creighton is intensely anti-American and highly critical of Quebec nationalism—it was met with criticism, but, as Donald Wright points out, *Canada's First Century* initially outsold *Everything You Always Wanted to Know About Sex* and, for a time, even the Bible.

Paperback | 416 pages | 6 x 9" | 9780195449228

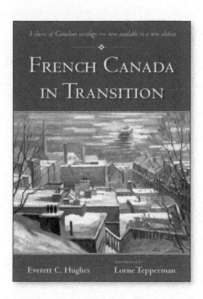

French Canada in Transition

Reissue

The late EVERETT HUGHES
Introduction by LORNE TEPPERMAN

"All Canadians should read this book."—*Canadian Journal of Economics and Political Science*

French Canada in Transition is a landmark study of the impact of rapid industrialization on small French Canadian communities. First published in 1943, it remains one of the most widely cited works of Canadian sociology. Hughes's careful study of a typical Quebec city revealed trends and developing fault lines that would only make themselves apparent to less perceptive observers two decades later with the flowering of the Quiet Revolution.

Paperback | 256 pages | 6 x 9" | 9780195429978